HEAVEN HELP THE HOME!

D1115778

HEAVEN
HELP
THE
HOME!

HOWARD G. HENDRICKS

While this book is intended for the reader's personal enjoyment
and profit, it is also intended for group study. A Leader's Guide
with Reproducible Response Sheets is available from your local
bookstore or from the publisher.

VICTOR BOOKS®

A DIVISION OF SCRIPTURE PRESS PUBLICATIONS INC.
USA CANADA ENGLAND

Scripture quotations in this book are from the *Authorized (King James) Version* (KJV) unless otherwise indicated. Other versions quoted include the *New American Standard Bible* (NASB), © the Lockman Foundation 1960, 1962, 1963, 1968, 1971, 1972, 1973, 1975, 1977; *The Living Bible* (TLB), © 1971, Tyndale House Publishers, Wheaton, IL 60189; *The New Testament in Modern English* (PH), Revised Edition, © J.B. Phillips, 1958, 1960, 1972, permission of Macmillan Publishing Co. and Collins Publishers; and the *Holy Bible, New International Version,* © 1973, 1978, 1984, International Bible Society. Used by permission of Zondervan Bible Publishers.

28   29   30   Printing/Year   94   93

Recommended Dewey Decimal Classification: 301.42
Suggested Subject Heading: MARRIAGE AND FAMILY

Library of Congress Catalog Card Number: 73-78689
ISBN: 0-88207-240-4

VICTOR BOOKS
A division of SP Publications, Inc.
Wheaton, Illinois 60187

Dedicated to

Barb, Bob, Bev, Bill

the four arrows God placed
in my quiver, uncommonly
gifted as my personal instruc-
tors in parenthood.

Contents

Preface

The Hendricks household was for twelve years enriched with a small, flop-eared, black dachshund named Franz. With immutable loyalty he helped rear our four irreverent and irascible children who vexed his early years with frustrations. Just when all four of them were grown, and Franz was settled into a dignified senior citizen routine compatible with his years, Fritz arrived.

Fritz was an eight-month-old German shepherd with a radical philosophy. For him the whole world was a delightful playground. He knew nothing about pecking order. He was a spoiled "only child," having lived with doting newlyweds since early puppyhood.

Confronted with this tall, handsome—but brash and unmannerly—stranger, our meek and mild Franz took charge. He did what had to be done. Calling forth some latent ferocity, he growled a basso profundo warning: "Get outa my food!" Fritz respectfully retired. Franz taught the shepherd when to bark, when—and when not—to relax in the dog house. The young whippersnapper learned to stay in his place! Amazingly, the monster dog, who could have pulverized the little licorice-colored headmaster with a clout of his paw, became a loyal companion, part of the team, an inseparable buddy.

This case history from the canine kingdom offered me a parabolic and instructive example. It is possible to overcome what seems like insuperable odds when your very survival may be at stake.

We are surrounded by foreign, hostile, and home-shattering influences in our world today. The supportive elements of society no longer feed and shade us. The Christian home must blossom in a field of weeds.

Our task then is to become a hardier breed, to function as a family with such virility that there is distinctive beauty in each Christian homegrown product. The means are at our disposal. Along with the church, God ordained the home; these are two divinely appointed organisms of human society. With the mandate to exist, God also provided the tools to function.

Heaven Help the Home is a guide to put these tools to work inside the home. It offers a plan of operation for the effective family that turns out durable, functional, and winsome people to represent Jesus Christ in a stormy age.

Living the Christian life is not flying by the seat of your pants. It is traveling a well-plotted course by means of fixed navigational aids. These stable, dependable markers jut out from the Scriptures, as I point out in these pages.

The causes of problems—not merely the symptoms—have pulled at my thinking. I desire that this book reach young parents whose child training lies ahead of them. It is very difficult to teach navigation in the middle of a storm!

The Christian home is a peculiar entity in a secular world. It is not *of* the world, but it is most assuredly *in* the world. Such a posture demands stamina and resistance, coupled with concern and interaction. Phillips paraphrases Paul (Rom. 12:2): "Don't let the world squeeze you into its mold." That is lethal conformity.

"Be of good cheer. I have overcome the world," Christ encourages believers (John 16:33). Of all the tasks we are given on this earth to perform, I believe there is not one with greater fulfillment than the building of a home that is Christ-approved. My reading of the Scriptures convinces me that God is saying to parents, "Right on!"

My ideas have moved along a circuitous route on their journey to this printed word. I am indebted to students and other patient listeners who originally tape-recorded my spoken thoughts.

My wife, Jeanne, however, is the one who mobilized these phrases and mustered them into a readable form with her well-articulated typewriter. Many insights in the manuscript are her unique contribution. Without her invaluable assistance, this book, as our family, could not be.

Howard G. Hendricks
Dallas, Texas

Introduction

Being an American father—and grandfather—whose years have spanned most of the twentieth century, I encounter some hazards in daring to put my thoughts about home life on paper. Nearly everybody, it is commonly assumed, who was born in the 1920s and grew up remembering the Great Depression is skewed toward an unrealistic view of today's families. Only 10 percent of American households now have a father as the single breadwinner, with mother and children at home. Life was simple "back then," I am told. The early telephones and motor cars, to say nothing of uncomplicated household appliances, gave people easy tracks to run on. Today, grandfathers are good for home-spun stories, but when plugged in to the high-speed, computerized lifestyle of our sophisticated world they fall short.

Bald heads and bifocals, however, are deceiving. My boyhood, unfortunately, is being relived thousands of times over in today's children. Historians who paint a scene of domestic tranquility for the "roaring twenties" may be the truly simplistic thinkers, because it was a decade of disaster for many like myself in the big city.

My parents eloped on a lark. Their homes seethed with the struggles of urban living, and I was most likely a compulsive mistake of their passions. The overflow of bad decisions continued to ripple, but the divorce did not happen until I was eighteen. The on-off separations began before I was born and, just like children today, I was a pawn on their adult chessboard; I got in the way. Reflecting on my past, I believe that I, more than ever, have earnest words to say to parents about what makes marriage and family work.

In the Christian world one of the most frequent emotions I meet is panic. Statistics on divorces, runaways, and abuses of all kinds have set us to questioning God. Some have reacted with extreme measures like escape into lifestyles of closed living and schooling. Many others, in a frantic attempt to outsmart the enemy, maintain as little interaction as possible with the world around. We are scared.

Since this book was first published, the phenomena of genetic engineering, a majority population of working mothers, and a general shift of values have forced families to ask new questions. We need not worry that God has been taken by surprise. His program is right on schedule, and His formula for the Christian family has not changed. I simply want to add some new data and to reinforce guidelines that He has given, reliable in any decade, in any century.

Howard G. Hendricks
December 1988

*Concern should be high
for home and family
because the world
turns on the home
and the church.*

ONE
Is the Christian Home
Safe for Occupancy?

"I've either got the wrong recipe or the wrong ingredients! I've thrown my whole life into this stew; and if this family isn't the worst mess of rotten goulash I've ever seen—well, I just wanna give up!"

This bitter blast spurted from Carolyn, twenty years down the holey road of marriage and motherhood. Carolyn grew up going to church and doing all the "right things." At the proper age she married Fred, a "really nice guy," generous, easygoing, and friendly. He was a bit weak, but she helped him make decisions.

When the two kids were born, Fred was gone most of the time in military service, but she managed. She even went to work to help save money for the home they would buy when he got out. When Fred came home, she intended to quit working, but he was restless, unsure of himself. So she kept on.

Soon it was apparent that Fred had a drinking problem. Typical for Carolyn, she was patient, understanding, and kept on running the job and the family. Meanwhile, Fred, on and off the job, in and out of hospitals, with and apart from his family, staggered through a decade of searching for solid ground.

"He's been living at home for about a year now," reported Carolyn, "and I think he finally knows he's always just a drink away from disaster. He's been doing pretty well, but I'm *really* worried now. Cari—that's our younger one—told us some time ago that when she graduates from high school next month, she plans to live with her boyfriend at the university. I thought somehow I'd talk her out of it. But I wasn't prepared for last night. When I got home from work, there was the truck (her boyfriend's pickup) moving all her stuff out of the house. She's just leaving! Going to live with that boy! I can't reason with her!"

The roofs that cover the Carolyns and Freds of our gasping twentieth-century culture are multiplying at alarming rates. The distinctively Christian home (not merely the home where Christians live, but where Christ lives) seems to be disappearing.

Should the Christian home advocates lay down arms and conclude it is a lost cause? Should we allow the historians to write that "the modular family unit characterized by monogamous marriage and adhering to the Judeo-Christian ethic saw its demise in the late twentieth century in the Western world"?

Why be concerned about the family? How important is the Christian home? Could we, maybe, just toss it out with the next garbage collection? Hardly! There are substantial and scriptural reasons which build a compelling and convincing case for the home.

The Bible Exalts the Family
We need to understand how prominent the family is in the Bible. God has much to say about marriage, sex, and the

family. This doctrine pervades the Word of God in both the Old and New Testaments. Somehow our churches too often save it for a Mother's Day special.

One superb showing of God's family portrait is inserted in Israel's ancient hymnbook, the Psalms.

> Unless the Lord builds the house,
> They labor in vain who build it;
> Unless the Lord guards the city,
> The watchman keeps awake in vain.
> It is vain for you to rise up early,
> To retire late,
> To eat the bread of painful labors;
> For He gives to His beloved even in his sleep.
>
> Behold, children are a gift of the Lord,
> The fruit of the womb is a reward.
> Like arrows in the hand of a warrior,
> So are the children of one's youth.
> How blessed is the man whose quiver is full of
>   them;
> They shall not be ashamed,
> When they speak with their enemies in the gate.
>   (Psalm 127, NASB)

The description begins with the foundation for the home. It starts with the *inception* and ends with the *impact* of the home. "Except the Lord build. . . ." The home begins with a philosophy, with a personal commitment. It is not saying you do not build your home—you do. Rather, it is a warning against the idiocy of trying to build your home alone. No way! You will never pull off the assignment as a Christian parent—as a partner in a dynamic relationship— without the Lord. You will never succeed even though you redouble your efforts by getting up earlier and staying up later. You will only ache, and there is no hurt comparable to the suffering of a failing parent. No amount of personal or professional success will compensate for parental bungling.

In this word picture of Psalm 127, God puts a blue ribbon on children. Look at His descriptive terms. He calls them a "heritage" or "gift." One authority says this word must be translated "assignment." Your children are God's assignment or commission, and He does not waste children on parents. He knows the very kind to send to you. Did you think God gave you children because of what you could do for them? That's only one part. He gave them because of what they could do for you. You can meet your children's particular needs and they can meet yours in a unique and special way.

The psalmic portrayal also calls children a "reward." Not a curse, not a tragedy, not an accident—they are the expression of God's favor. It is a thrilling sight to see your children through the lens of Scripture as His trophies.

Now I hear someone saying, "What happens to the couple who does not have children?" Though children are the obvious reward of the Lord upon a marriage, it does not follow that if you do not have children, He is not rewarding you. God has many creative means of rewarding His children.

If babies are born into your home, you are highly honored. If, in the providence of God, you do not have children, then God has an altogether different and unique plan for you. You may discover the most distinctive ministry you have ever experienced in life—building into the lives of children whose parents couldn't care less. Some of us are here only because somebody else cared for us more than our parents did.

Children are also called "arrows." That presupposes that they are to be launched toward a target—and that you know what the target is. One major reason parents fail is they have never sighted the target.

Talk to the teens in the average church youth group about their parents. You get a graphic replay of adult activity—often frenzied, directionless, reminiscent of the definition of a fanatic (one who redoubles his efforts *after* he has lost sight of his goal!)

Good children don't emerge by accident; they are the fruit of careful cultivation. Make raising good children your clear-cut objective, the specific aim for which you are trusting God.

Society Depends on the Family
Concern should be high for home and family because the world turns on the home and the church. These are two divinely appointed agencies recognized in the New Testament.

A church bulletin listed activities for every night of the week. The pastor placed it under my nose and said, "Look at that, Hendricks, something going every night!"

"Are you proud of that?" I asked. "I wouldn't be. What if some family wanted to build their home life? On exactly what night of the week would you suggest they do this?"

The disturbing question rises: is it possible that some churches are doing more to break up homes than to build them? Are we engaged in a program of competition with the home, or cooperation? Do churches conceive of the home as an adversary or an ally?

Most Christians spend a great deal of their lives in parachurch groups. Two tests should be applied to any such group: Does it emphasize the importance of the church? Does it emphasize the importance of the home? In many churches today the two are almost diametrically opposed. The home simply provides the church with "customers." In contrast, we are suggesting a church should be primarily committed to training parents to do the work God has called *them* to do, not trying to do their work for them. The chief job of the home, as conceived by God, is to train the family members to live fruitfully in home, church, and society.

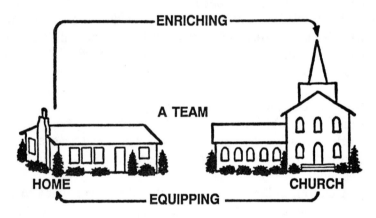

God's personnel officer, the Holy Spirit, tacks up His requirements for applicants to the deacon and elder posts in 1 Timothy 3. Very high on the list in both cases is effective functioning in the family—"one who rules well." Because how can you rule the church if you can't rule your home? If you cannot serve well in a limited sphere, don't enlarge it. If we are looking for a person qualified for leadership in the church, we are not to look at his public ministry only but also at his management in his home. If he cannot function in his home, then he has forfeited the privilege of leadership in the church.

On a flight from San Francisco to Chicago, I was seeking, as always, an opportunity to share my faith. I was seated next to a young business executive with a small corporation headquartered in Chicago. It seemed the time was ripe to broach spiritual things, but the minute I did he bristled.

"Would you mind if we changed the subject?" he asked curtly.

"Not at all," I replied, "but I'd be interested to know why."

"I'll tell you why I'm not interested in Christianity," he said. "Christianity robbed me of my parents, and I'm not interested in anything that would do that." Then he told me a sordid story of a father who traveled rather extensively as a Christian businessman giving his testimony, and of a mother who was busily engaged in teaching home Bible classes. Then he added with a touch of sarcasm and bitterness, "My parents were so busy leading everyone else to Christ that they lost their four boys, and there's not one of us who's interested. Now, would you mind if we changed the subject!"

I remember the day Jeanne and I sat down and drove a stake into our own marriage. We agreed that prominence as a professor, or a writer, or a speaker, or even a homemaker, would never supplant being known as a godly parent in our own family. You don't think God ignores a commitment like that, do you?

Succeeding in church and failing at home can be a copout. One spends more and more time at church where he or she is "making it," and less and less time at home where there is static. God says that if you cannot conduct your home life, don't try to lead in a public ministry. Actually, you have nothing to say.

The average church has a child 1 percent of his time; the home has him 83 percent of the time; and the school for the remainder. We are too often trying to do in our churches on a 1-percent basis what we cannot accomplish. We are neglecting this choice 83-percent period when children are exposed to parents on a very dynamic interpersonal level. The home marks a child for life.

Columbia University spent a quarter of a million dollars in research, only to corroborate the truth of Scripture. Conclusion: there is no second force in the life of a child compared with the impact of his home. The compelling crisis today is the training and equipping of parents to do the job.

Society Assaults the Family

Concern for the home is mandatory in the severe climate of contemporary society. Nobody lives in a vacuum. We breathe the air of a world that is sensual, secular, and incredibly unscrupulous. We cannot escape its contagion. It rubs off on us and on our children.

God's orthopedic clinic, Ephesians 4–6, tells Christians to "walk circumspectly," that is, looking all around. Looking around, what do we see? *Seventeen*, the girls' magazine that once was devoted to clothes, cosmetics, and calorie counting, has added areas with moral implications. One issue included an advice piece on abortion and another story with this subtitle, "You can't tell about a man until you're in troubled water with him." Every parent should mentally slip into daughter's shoes and think of reading these from the teen viewpoint.

A morning newspaper ran a series on criminal assaults on women. This statement was included: "The typical rapist is likely to look more like a young bank executive, clean-shaven, well-dressed, and somewhat charming." What are the implications for our young people? Is the rapist really a nice guy after all?

Time reports weekly on scandals, assassinations, abuses,

and all varieties of wrongdoing which seem to be tolerated in our world. Relative to a large corporate takeover, an editor wrote: "The size of the deal and the fortunes to be made appear to exceed any foreseeable benefits to U.S. industry." Our children live in a world where black hats are winning more often than "the good guys."

In such an atmosphere, how do we train our children? Do we put our heads piously in the sand, hoping everything bad will go away?

Last spring two beautiful red cardinals came to our backyard. They mated, built a nest in a small pyracantha tree, and flourished in the quiet beauty of their secluded home. The female laid five eggs. She sat on them faithfully every day, and we watched with fascination. One day, very surreptitiously, a thief came along. We believe it was probably a squirrel—just during a short time the mother was gone. Four eggs were stolen and the nest disheveled. When we came out the door, both cardinals were sitting on the fence very close to the gate, though they had been very distant previously. They were extremely agitated, chirping and chattering as if to sound an SOS or perhaps to scold us for their tragic dilemma. Their home was ruined and their family aborted.

What a picture of many Christian homes where parents look the other way, failing to realize the enemy is at hand.

Sometimes we tend to think of the "big problems" as outside the church, but unfortunately most social problems have infected the churches and the lives of church people. In our community a young girl in an evangelical church became pregnant. She attended youth group on Sunday night, and Monday she caught a plane for New York City. Tuesday she entered a hospital. Wednesday she aborted the baby. Thursday she was in convalescence. Friday she took the plane back to Dallas. Sunday she was back in the youth group—and no one knew she had been pregnant or that she had an abortion.

Later, she came for counseling, covered with guilt. The real issue was uncovered. It was a cover-up for her parents—an active father, on the board of the church, and a mother quite busy in a teaching ministry connected with the church. Both of them compelled her to go to New York for the abortion, and the girl was not convinced this was what she should do. Such things do not only happen "outside" Christian circles.

Christianity Needs the Family

The most vital concern for the home springs from the fact that it is the most dynamic means of perpetuating virile Christianity. A Christian home stands out in bold relief in a pagan society. Paul wrote to Timothy, "Continue thou in the things which thou hast learned" (2 Tim. 3:14). What things? The answer is in 2 Timothy 1:5, "the unfeigned faith that is in thee, which dwelt first in thy grandmother, Lois, and thy mother, Eunice." Timothy was a third-generation Christian. He was handpicked by the Apostle Paul to be his associate.

Now and then someone says, "I'd rather see a person who didn't come from a Christian home, but from paganism, and then came to know Christ, because of the excitement of his newfound faith." There is only one problem to that: it is contrary to Scripture.

We have discovered at Dallas Seminary great limitations in the preponderance of men who do not come from Christian homes. Many men sit across my desk from me who are committed wall-to-wall, deeply in love with Jesus Christ, but who say, "Prof, I can't get it all together." A Christian home provides the greatest foundation upon which to build a life and ministry.

One of the most exciting things about working and ministering in this generation is to see the steady stream of young men and women who come to trust Christ, and whose primary purpose and passion in life is to provide distinctively Christian homes for their children. Down through the years the greatest source of leadership in the evangelical church has been the Christian home. The disappearance of such homes from the scene is a very alarming trend. It ought to stab us awake. It ought to commit us to the proposition that the Lord must build the house. We'll never pull it off. There is no Plan B. God has committed Himself to this. The question is, have you?

*Roles always
determine relationships,
and relationships
create responsibility.*

TWO

Performing the Art
of Family Living

Good relationships—it seems everybody wants them, but where does one place an order? What Christian bookstore handles them? Do you have to take special training to qualify? Apply for a license? Are they inherited? Many of us are not even sure what a good relationship is.

A blight which used to occur only rarely is doing unprecedented damage to American homes. "I don't need you in my life," is the message which has triggered an epidemic of failing families. The National Center for Missing and Exploited Children in Washington, D.C. listed more than 1.5 million names in 1985. Currently it is estimated that as many as 2 million American children are displaced—runaways, abandoned, abused.

Our daughter Bev was in her freshman psychology class a thousand miles and two months away from home. The professor said that it is normal for children to reject their parents. "In fact," he said, "most of you kids would probably tell me that you hate your homes. There is a sense in which you *should* reject it all. . . ."

Bev was out of breath as she grabbed the first opportunity to get to the phone. "Mom? Dad? I'm just fine, and I've got to tell you that I really love you, and I don't reject you. You probably think I'm crazy to be telling you this, but our teacher said we are normal if we hate our homes, and I *don't. . . .*"

So common has it become for parents and children to reject each other that this professor was setting it up as normative living. He was saying that it's proper for the domestic train to be derailed, for the bearing to get hot, for the coupling to break.

I believe that God has an infinitely better and more workable plan for the family—mutually satisfying and productive of good relationships.

God displayed His model home in the Garden of Eden. He said it was *not good* that Adam should be alone. Remember, Adam had the friendly companionship of all the animal life. He lived in the plushest environment ever known—no ecological problems there! He even enjoyed the presence of God Himself. But God said something was lacking. And God created Eve to form the first family. That family, God said, was *good.*

Adam and Eve were commanded by God to have children. This was the divine design—to live in families with children. Only disobedience to God ruptured the relationship. Sin drove our first parents from the garden. Sin motivated the murder of Abel by his older brother, Cain. Sin disrupted family life then, and the pattern continues today. Any sociologist will confirm that children from "bad" homes usually make "bad" marriages, which in turn produce more "bad" homes.

Dr. Harold Voth, senior psychiatrist at the Menninger Foundation, Topeka, Kansas, has written: "The cycle of sick or weak people who are the product of sick or broken families keeps repeating itself, the effects spread from one generation to the next and slowly but surely the sickness tears down the best tradition of mankind which made our society strong" (preface, *The Castrated Family*, p. xiii, Sheed Andrews and McMeel, Inc., 1977).

How does one break this vicious cycle? How does one convert bad to good? "It has something to do with love." That's what people will tell you when you ask. It's a persistent thread that keeps running through all civilizations—the power of love.

Ancient biblical literature surfaced it. Proverbs says, "Hatred stirs up strife, but *love* covers all transgressions" (10:12, NASB). The Song of Solomon proclaims, "His banner over me is *love*" (2:4, NASB).

Where did the concept of love originate? The Prophet Jeremiah told the people of Israel through his tears that God loved them "with an everlasting love" (31:3, NASB). But the full explanation comes from the New Testament. The Apostle John said that God *is* love, and that we love Him because He first loved us. "Let us love one another, for love is of God" (1 John 4:7-8).

Do you love God? "Of course, every Christian loves God," you reply. OK. If we love God, then we must obey God. The Apostle John writes it negatively, "Anyone who does not do what is right is not a child of God; nor is anyone who does not love his brother" (1 John 3:10, NIV). That's where the home begins. A man and a wife, each love-related to God through His Son, who is the expression of God's love to man. Each related to the other in human love and mutual trust.

The strength of this triangle is invincible. The closer each partner moves toward God, the closer he or she is to the other. Closeness brings into focus the other person, and knowing who God is helps us find out who we are.

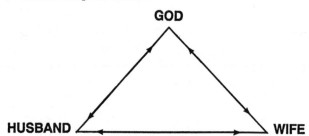

Perhaps this explains why God often has to back us into a crisis corner where we can see only Him before we get ourselves into perspective. A discernment of roles is absolutely indispensable for purposeful living, for marital efficiency, and for family functioning.

Roles? What roles? Sometimes they are almost lost in the pollution of mixed-up people, for we are living in a society in which marital roles are brutally blurred. In fact, there are many who are convinced that there is no basic difference between man and woman except biological. With the advancement of science, these people say, even this will be thoroughly blended.

Now I want to set before you a basic principle. *Roles always determine relationships, and relationships create responsibility.*

Ephesians tells how to live a heavenly life in a hellish world. The first three chapters are the theological foundation, and the last three are the experiential superstructure. Nestled in this intensely practical, second section is a passage dealing with roles and relationships, and the responsibilities of husband and wife (5:22-29). There are two main strands: the husband's position and his passion.

The Husband as Head
The husband is described as the head of the home. That lends *authority* to the relationship.

The context here is extremely crucial. Verse 18 says, "And be not drunk with wine wherein is excess, but be filled with the Spirit." What does the filling of the Spirit produce? How will I *know* when I'm under the Spirit's control? That is not as hard to determine as some would have you believe. There are clear-cut distinguishable marks, and it is significant functioning in the family in one's divinely designed role that is the first proof positive of Spirit control. Verse 21 really comprises the topic phrase: "Submitting yourselves one to another in the fear of God."

Submission is not the exclusive responsibility of the woman. Submission is the lifestyle of the Christian. To the woman, the question is, are you willing to submit yourself, not first of all to your husband, but to the Lord's plan for your functioning in marital relationship? Don't let anybody fog you. If you cannot submit to your husband's leadership, then your problem is not only with your husband. Your problem is also with your Lord. You have not faced the basic issue of the lordship of Christ. The filling of the Holy Spirit always involves submission to Christ.

Our first task is to blast before we can build. Let's excise from our minds some wormy ideas about headship.

1. The husband is not dictator.
A lot of frustrated sergeants are running around with biblical club in hand shouting, "I'm the head of my home."

You know they're not; if they were, they'd never have to tell you.

Often, when I speak on this subject, I get the distinct impression that some woman is sitting there saying, "That's right, my husband is the head, and I'm the neck that moves the head!" Because the real issue is not who rules the roost, but who rules the rooster!

"The husband is the head of the wife *as* Christ also is the head of the church" (Eph. 5:23, NASB). Christ is not in the process of cramming anything down His bride's (the church's) throat. Neither should a scripturally enlightened husband be. If he is, it is not only because he does not understand the Word, but also because he has a lot of personal emotional problems for which this supposed leadership is really a cover.

2. The husband is not superior.

The Word of God teaches that in Christ male and female do not exist. Galatians 3:28 says there is neither male nor female, bond nor free—all are one. But being equal spiritually does not mean we all have the same functions. We are equal spiritually but different functionally. And the functional distinction has been determined by God, who created marriage and the functioning relationship. To distort those functions is to devastate the relationship.

This principle comes into full bloom in the life of Abraham and Sarah. Spiritually they are equal. The history lesson in Hebrews 11 states very clearly that *Sarah herself* received strength . . . because *she* judged Him faithful who had promised. Even unbelieving Sarah came to faith, and God equated her faith with Abraham's. Functionally, Abraham was the load-bearing member of the team. God interviewed Abraham, not Sarah, to brief him on the divine itinerary for their lives. Abraham functioned as the head of the home.

"But I would have you know that the head of every man is Christ; and the head of the woman is the man; and the head of Christ is God" (1 Cor. 11:3). Jesus Christ had a function on earth, a God-given function designed in the eternal council. He would be born of a woman, live, suffer, and die the ignominious death of a cross. In complete and loving obedience to His Father's will, Jesus Christ submitted Himself to that plan. Does that mean that Jesus Christ is inferior to God? My friend, that is blasphemy! And it is also heresy to say that to be in submission to your husband casts you into an inferior role.

Think it through carefully, wives. Your whole life rests on this issue. If you want God's blessing on your home, there is no alternate route. You function by His design. I didn't invent it. Paul didn't dream it up—and don't charge him with having an antifeminine bias! This is God's plan, and if you want God's blessing, you will have to function by God's specifications. You will never find fulfillment apart from it.

3. The husband is not the exclusive decision-maker.

This comes out over and over in question-and-answer sessions. "You mean to tell me that if my husband is the head of our family he's going to make *all* the decisions?"

No husband in his right mind even attempts to make all decisions without delegation. May I remind you that Jesus Christ—think of it—Jesus Christ has delegated to the church the carrying out of His mission on earth. That's the confidence the Saviour has in us! And that's the confidence a husband must place in his wife.

It is utterly ridiculous for me to make decisions in areas in which I am totally incompetent, but in which my wife is extremely gifted and capable. I am willing and eager to encourage her to make decisions in areas for which I have no expertise. But I am the one responsible under God for decisions made, whether I make them or she makes them.

4. The husband is not always right.

Whether a husband is right or not, he is responsible. He is a pacesetter, a decision-maker; he takes the initiative. He is not passively acquiescent but actively deciding. God will never hold a wife responsible for a poor decision the husband made but He will hold her responsible for failure to submit. We're not talking about a perfect relationship. We're talking about people. And whenever you've got people you've got problems. Husbands are not omniscient, any more than wives are.

What we must do is build marriage on the basis of strengths, not on liabilities. We are all going to make mistakes—that way we know we are in the club! But every time a wife looks at her husband she ought to feel respect. He is the one who has to answer to God for leadership in the home. When a wife gets to heaven, the Lord will never say, "You sure did a bad job in leading that family." The only thing He will ask is how she functioned on the basis of the role He gave her.

Many a man is a leader in public and a washout at home. A young wife told me recently, "My father was a leader in every area except in the family."

Wives, let me hit you with a challenge: are you making it easier or harder for your husband to function in his role? Often a woman comes up with: "My husband just won't function as a leader." Really? Is it that he won't take the leadership, or that you won't yield it to him? Or, in the face of stubborn resistance, are you willing to walk through a wobbly period of transition so that he can learn by doing?

The Husband: Leader and Lover

In Ephesians 5:25-29, the phrase is repeated twice, "Husbands, love your wives even as Christ also loved the church." The husband is to be the head of the home; he is also to be the heart of the home. It is his headship which provides authority; it is his heart that provides affection. One without the other always leads to distortion. He is to be a leader; he is to be a lover.

If the husband is a leader without being a lover, he is an autocratic individual; if he is a lover without being a leader, he will be a sentimentalist. If he has leadership with love, no woman in her right mind resists placing herself willingly and submissively under a man who loves as Christ loves the church. Christ's example is obedience to the Father, "full of grace and truth," never reinforcing weakness, always insisting on honesty and purity.

I had a student come to me and say, "I have a problem. I love my wife too much."

I blinked. "Run that by again. I hear it so seldom." I took him to the Ephesians passage: "love your wife as Christ also loved the church."

"Do you love her that much?" I asked.

"Oh, no, of course not!"

I said, "Get with it!"

Loving one's wife is a full-time assignment. It takes every ounce of creativity a man has to pour himself into this person God has brought into his life, "to love as Christ also loved the church and gave Himself for it" (Eph. 5:25).

Christ died for the church. He also allowed it to suffer in order to strengthen it. The present-day palaver about never hurting anyone you love is far from the truth. Love will always *do what is best* for the loved one. You ought to thank God if you have a mate who is willing to say, "Dear, there is a problem. . . ." You have someone who loves you enough to be concerned about your relationship.

"So ought men to love their wives as their own bodies" (Eph. 5:28). That's what a wife is—an extension. What an assignment! Wives, do you think submission is a task? Run this one by! That's what God is holding your husband responsible for—to be your leader, your lover. Are you making it easier for him to lead you, to love you? Or harder?

The Relationship of Parents and Children

That little other person came into our home—very subtly. At first there was no one else, just us two. Then all the indications pointed toward—something. The doctor called it a pregnancy. We called it a baby. Think of it—*our* baby. She was born warm and wiggly—hungry—for food and attention. We shared eagerly. We cared very much about everything she did. She never asked, "Who am I?" She knew she was ours, the object of our love, the living proof of our one-flesh relationship. And we taught her that God loves her more than we do—much more.

Loved, wanted, cared for—most children in normal homes start out that way. What happens to fray and so often break the bonds of kinship during the tattered teen years? Why does a parent so often resent the bold presence of his children a mere ten years or so after he has welcomed them so warmly into the world?

The Bible assumes that children are naturally to be loved and cared for. There are no long exhortations in Scripture about loving children, but the implications abound—like so many green plants adding vitality to the biblical decor (2 Tim. 3:15; Titus 2:4, for example).

When parents love God, they love each other, and they love their children. The children naturally respond with love for parents and for each other. This love is the *good* relationship. This love is God's plan.

Someone has observed, "When the naturalist violates the laws of nature, he gets chaos; when the parent ignores God's plan for human life, he gets distortion of some sort or other."

Blended Families

In reality, every family is a blend, a combination of one-time strangers who moved into the orbit of friendship and eventually members of a common household. The brittleness of families today, however, prompts frequent fractures and the consequence is a large number of rejoined family groups where stepparents and step-siblings are called to adjust to each other.

Several years ago my wife and I were invited into such a home. Both parents had been married previously and had children; each had suffered through a painful divorce and their seven children were all affected by feelings of rejection and apprehension. Yet as we met each child, ranging in age from preschool to college-age, a remarkable team spirit and upbeat optimism was evident. The parents shared with us some of the secrets of blending families successfully. I have added some additional thoughts, and I call them the bylaws of blending:

1. Plan the strategy of the merger. When two existent families come together, every member must be considered. Each relationship must be examined so that each cross-connection is understood and considered sympathetically. The new love between mother and father must be explained and gently extended with patience and acceptance.

2. Put a family agreement in writing. This document should account for each family member as a contributing part of a new team. Rights and responsibilities, limitations and rewards, every facet of home life which can be anticipated should be noted and signed by everyone.

3. Practice reevaluation. Daily routine tends to wear down good intentions. A regular family council is a good preventive for deteriorating attitudes. Each person should be encouraged to express his or her feelings; problems need to be discussed. Embarrassment and put-downs should be disallowed; all assets and liabilities must be shared. Obviously, leadership is required and that belongs to the parents.

4. Clarify authority and access to it. Families vary in their organization according to temperaments and abilities, but everyone needs to understand who is in charge and what to do with problems, criticism, and dissatisfaction. They all need to learn respect for each other and ways to resolve conflict, all in the process of learning the meaning of love.

5. Employ the tool of family worship. Nothing smooths relationships and nourishes a home more than a time of common adoration of God and prayer for needs which everyone shares. There is no greater stabilizer or healer of hurts. The warmth that is generated in loving God together prevents problems and supplies reassurance of a bonding that goes with an individual throughout life.

Relating to children in the home as a parent is not only *doing;* it is also *being.* Like a diligent spider spinning a delicate web strand by strand, the parent must give of himself with singleness of purpose to produce strong rapport. In the process he also receives from the child so that mutual trust is established.

One wise man has said that parents can create a favorable climate for children, but only experiences consolidate the learning. What kind of experiences are you having? Do they build or destroy the parent-child relationship? Let me give you some standards for measurement.

1. Practice a sincere respect for the child's worth as an individual. Does he speak to you? He speaks as long as you will listen. Listening far surpasses lecturing as a method of training. If your child does not talk to you, he has had his "off" button pushed somewhere in the past.

You may have read reports of the tragic autistic children—those little ones who have attempted to end communication with their world by refusing to speak or to react in any way. This state is the extreme, but moving in the same direction to a lesser degree are many other children who are closing doors and windows on their world because they have been told too often, "Be quiet." "Hush up." "Go away."

2. Provide your child's basic needs. Don't provide all his wants or your frustrated desires for him, but his needs: privacy, a place to play and study, clean clothes, ownership of his own things, time to be alone, a sensible program of eating and exercise, opportunity to make appropriate decisions. Always tell him the truth.

3. Expose children to real-life experiences. Use births, marriages, deaths, and disasters as teaching times. You will help her both to satisfy her curiosity and avoid irrational fears.

My wife visited the site of a plane crash in her early years. She was full of questions, and her childish imagination ran rampant as she viewed the wreckage scattered over the ground. An uncle explained to her, in simple terms, some of the reasons such tragedies occur. He explained the importance of good training and obeying the laws of nature and aviation. It was a simple conversation, but a lifetime buffer for a little girl who might otherwise have been warped by the sight of bloody horror.

Make the child aware by issuing realistic warnings against danger. Build resources into the child with prayer and private talks, with a growing familiarity and trust of the Bible as a standard, and with exposure to trustworthy adults.

4. Help the child set goals by discussing possible objectives. For example, many children from Christian homes make a commitment of their lives to Jesus Christ. The parents often comment favorably, but do little to implement the decision. The young person needs to discuss what is involved in the decision. She should be exposed to those who have followed a similar life pattern. This is discipleship. She needs to discover what in-between steps must be taken to reach her goal. In moving toward all goals, by all means allow for failures, and encourage, encourage, encourage!

5. *Teach the child the how-to of daily life so that he may function without frustration.* Confidence grows in the soil of doing it yourself. We laugh at the girl who cannot drive a car properly, the boy who can't get his own breakfast, the man who is lost without his wife to match his ties and socks. Seldom do we consider the frustration that hobbles these individuals. Nobody ever took the time to teach them.

A child should be taught to do as much by himself as he can handle. This builds confidence and contributes to safety. The toddler who is taught to use the telephone with serious intent—not as a toy—has been given a tool that will be useful for a lifetime.

Performance, however, must be on his own level. Don't expect more than he can possibly produce. Are you a dad who loses patience with his son because he did not score the touchdown? Are you a mother who refuses to speak to her daughter because she did not arrange her hair as requested? Such parents produce frustrations that push children in the direction of just giving up.

6. *Fences lend security for emotional development.* Set reasonable limits for the child's behavior. Just as surely as the backyard fence protects in a physical way, behavioral limits shield the young person from the fear of not knowing when to stop. Complementary to setting limits are the warnings about dangers of traffic, fire, drugs, plastic bags—all the many traps of childhood. Such concern tells the child that his parents care very much what happens to him.

Things NEVER, NEVER (well, hardly ever) to do!

Don't threaten—you decimate your own authority.

Don't bribe—bargaining usually makes you the loser.

Don't lose your temper—a clear demonstration of lack of control.

Don't refuse to explain—they'll go elsewhere and you're on the outside.

Don't use sarcasm or embarrassment—the fastest way to demolish a relationship.

Don't dash their dreams—your ticket into the generation gap.

If a child lives with criticism, says Dr. Haim Ginott, he does not learn responsibility. He learns to condemn himself and to find fault with others. He learns to doubt his own judgment, to disparage his own ability, and to distrust the intentions of others. Above all, he learns to live with continual expectation of impending doom.

A prominent Christian psychiatrist conducted interviews with a large number of young children who had taken hallucinogenic drugs. One reason given for taking the drugs was an extreme dissatisfaction with themselves and their relationships with others. This same doctor sampled 1,500 college dropouts. He reported two outstanding characteristics: (1) marked isolation from their parents, especially fathers; and (2) overwhelming, paralyzing apathy, complete lack of motivation.

When a child lives with parents who believe in her, she instinctively holds a higher view of herself and of her brothers and sisters as well. Everybody's sense of worth is enhanced.

There will be inevitable squabbling among children; it is in their nature. It is also the polishing process to prepare young people to mix and match in the adult world ahead. Parents need to distinguish between the superficial, normal sparking as young personalities touch live wires together, and the deep, smoldering hatred that may burn out a relationship for life. Brothers and sisters need each other, but they are individuals in their own right, and should be recognized as such.

Peel off the film which may be obscuring a higher view of your home. In a *Reader's Digest* article titled "Perfect Home," Norman Corwin wrote of children in these terms: "One child makes a home a course in liberal education for both himself and parents; two children make it a private school; three or more make it a campus. . . . All in all, the home is the great staging ground for the family's traffic with the world, as well as a fortress against the world's intrusions."

Single Adult Children
A phenomenon of Western world culture today is the large number of children who grow up and never leave home, postponing marriage or deciding against it. Many choose to live apart from their parents for a while and then return home. One recent study reported that among twenty-five to twenty-nine-year-olds, 16 percent of the men and 11 percent of women have returned to or had never left their parents' home. Young adults actually supported by their parents has reached a thirty-year high (*Dallas Morning News*, July 20, 1988, from *Current Population Reports*). Sociologists explain that reasons are unclear, but delays in marriage, early divorces, increases in housing costs, and a backfiring of permissive child-rearing styles may account for the situation.

Whatever the reason, the Christian family which includes a young single adult needs to see itself as a responsible team. In the Gospels Jesus Christ interacted with His friends Mary, Martha, and Lazarus, teaching them the importance of maintaining love and proper priorities.

At one time in our family, our older son Bob returned home after having been living independently. Although he was still our much-loved son, intergenerational differences were evident. We had to come to an adult understanding about the use of cars, kitchen, and all the household facilities. We respected his rights as an adult; and he agreed that this was still the home of Mom and Dad, and their wishes would be given preference. Again, the important thread of good communication woven in early years held us together in a workable harmony.

In-laws

One of our children arrived home from college one day with an announcement: wedding plans were in our future. One person made a decision but all of us were affected. The Hendricks family had received notice that we were going to have another member. True, this once casual acquaintance had spent the night, eaten at our table, visited with us, and won our affections. But were we ready to make him part of the inner circle?

In-laws are intruders. They may or may not be truly welcome, but they come into a family with legal sanction. They are binding. Most often they are not pre-loved; we have to learn to appreciate them. They are essentially transplants from an alien culture, competitors for support and resources, a responsibility assigned without a vote. We Americans have always disliked taxation without representation.

As Christians we need to disarm ourselves and pursue loving détente. I'd like to suggest three disarmament strategies:

1. Preplanning—warm, trusting relationships between parents and children tend to guide marriage choices toward those whom all will love.

2. Prayer—sharing with a child from youngest years, in prayer times, expectations that God will bring His choice of a partner places marriage in the province of the Holy Spirit's direction.

3. Positive friendship—families which build warm friendships with the in-laws reap bountiful harvests of mutual support and respect.

In-law relationships take time to settle in. The blending of two families tends to stir prejudice and bias. The commonest areas of disagreement, grandchildren, possessions, decisions about a place of residence, time together, treatment of illnesses, and religious preferences, among many, need to be dealt with realistically and sensitively. Dr. Joyce Brothers (*Dallas Morning News*, November 30, 1986) stated, "Usually when someone has difficulty adjusting to in-laws, it's because the person hasn't ever fully made the break with his or her own parents." There's a clue: we need to prepare our children to leave us, to give them the freedom to love a partner, fully assured that we will continue loving and supporting. Our willingness to let go frees them in turn to maintain warm ties with home and parents. The real payoff comes as senior years approach. Grown children and grandchildren who truly respect and appreciate aging parents are the best social security we can have.

The Extended Family
The constellation of the family often includes satellite members. In addition to parents and children, grandparents, aunts, uncles, and cousins sometimes are part of day-to-day living. What is the proper role and relationship of this extended family?

A plaintive note is frequently sounded when relatives are discussed. "I'd really like to be closer with her, but we live in two different worlds."

How is it that two people who were possibly very close in earlier years can drift far apart? Proximity on the family tree has very little to do with the nearness one feels to relatives. Friendship must be nurtured, and the Christian especially has a responsibility to maintain a healthy relationship with members of his or her own family as a testimony to the power of Christ in daily life.

One woman complains: "We had a pretty serious squabble, my sister and I, twenty years ago, over a boyfriend. She married him; I left." A kinship that was once close split and has remained fractured for years. Since then this woman has come to trust Christ. How does she mend a rift like that?

Bridges can be built across the most troubled waters when Christ is the motivator. It may require an apology that you said you would never make. It may call for a humility of spirit that is beyond human effort. With eternal perspective, however, the irritations of life shrink to proper size. Paul reminds us, "I can do all things through Christ" (Phil. 4:13).

Even after twenty years a birthday card with a simple inscription—"I think of you on this day every year (and lots in between)—just thought I'd let you know"—can be a bridge.

Distance sometimes makes mending easier. The hardest friendships to build are sometimes under the same roof. Harder, yet in many ways easier. There are more opportunities. A moment to say, "Please forgive me. I'm really sorry about what happened." An opportunity to give: "Why don't you let me help you with that?" These are bridges, built beam by beam to cross an emotional ravine—to mend, heal, and love for Christ's sake.

Increasingly, one of the thorniest problems is the inclusion of grandparents in a family.

A poignant picture is sketched in Israel's ancient history. The Book of Ruth records the story of a young Moabitish widow who left her family, her homeland, and her religious beliefs to devote herself to her beloved mother-in-law Naomi. Naomi *earned* the love and the loyalty of Ruth.

Look closely at that relationship. Naomi achieved fulfillment in her later years by submerging her personal interests in deference to Ruth. She ordered her life in a pattern which helped the younger generation. She remained active, contributory, and she died a happy and satisfied woman.

Naomi stands as a worthy model for all mothers-in-law, so unselfishly opening her heart to her son's wife that a lifetime merger of love was cemented between them.

Two principles concerning roles and relationships apply to having in-laws live with a family.

1. Both Old and New Testaments teach that parents are to be loved, supported, and cared for by the children (Ex. 20:12; Lev. 20:9; implied in James 2:14-20). Paul wrote boldly to Timothy, "If any provide not for his own, and specially for those of his own house, he hath denied the faith, and is worse than an infidel" (1 Tim. 5:8).

2. When a new family unit is established, its integrity must not be diluted by parental intrusion. Scripture says, "For this cause shall a man *leave father and mother* and shall cleave to his wife" (Matt. 19:5, emphasis mine). If it becomes necessary for older parents to move into an established family unit of one of their children, they should not expect to resume parental control, but should take a submerged role in the spirit of Naomi.

With these principles to guide, it seems clear when a family must decide how and where an older parent is to live, the father of that family must lead in making the decision. He has a scriptural mandate to see that his parents and the parents of his wife are cared for when the need arises. How? That depends on individual factors.

Ideally, a man and his wife should pray and discuss the situation before a decision is made. What is best for the individual? What is best for the family? This is a time to be coldly practical, yet warmly loving.

Americans increasingly discriminate against old people in what has been termed "ageism." One psychiatrist says, "Ageism is just not wanting to have all these ugly old people around. But in modern America, family units are small, the generations live apart, and social changes are so rapid that to learn about the past is considered irrelevant."

Anthropologist Margaret Mead calls old people "a strangely isolated generation, the carriers of a dying culture."

Grandparents

Ever since social security deductions became a reality in most American paychecks, the retired and aging person has been viewed through a curtain of dollar signs. In former generations older family members settled in with the closest relative and were generally accepted for whatever contributions they could make. Nowadays the ailing oldster who can no longer work and support himself is the object of a cruel question, can we afford you? (Or, if the individual has prudently accrued a nest egg, how much can we get out of you?) Senior citizen care can be very expensive.

As of September 1988 the U.S. Census Bureau recorded nearly 7 million Americans over age eighty. As the second fastest population growth group, there will be twice that many by the year 2050. Does God intend that our landscape be dotted with rest homes for the elderly by then? The Scriptures explain that God has numbered our days; He takes us home when He is ready. Until then He seems to be telling us to keep busy and productive. Psalm 92:14, speaking of the righteous, says "They will still bear fruit in old age, they will stay fresh and green" (NIV). Obviously, the psalmist is not describing bodies but minds. Our thinking is to remain active and vital. The Swiss psychologist, Dr. Paul Tournier, says, "The fact is that in order to make a success of old age, we must raise our culture-level; and this must be done well before we are old. But that necessarily implies a value judgment about culture, about the meaning of culture, and lastly about the meaning of our lives—a religious question *par excellence.*"

To understand how a modern individual remains alive mentally, we must face realistically what deadens the mind and what nourishes it. The well-known command to the Romans, "Be transformed by the renewing of your mind" (12:2, NIV) and to the Colossians, "Set your minds on the things above" (3:1, NASB) clues us that the pull of worldly concerns has a downward and deadening influence. Christ relieves anxiety; He rejuvenates the spirit. To the Philippians Paul wrote, "Do not be anxious about anything. The peace of God which transcends all understanding will guard your hearts and your minds in Christ Jesus" (4:6-7, NIV).

Two important principles which concern grandparents are threaded through the Bible. First, God sees mankind as His family, in a connected line. Age is secondary to family relationships. Second, a crucial message needs to be delivered, that of God's love through His Son. Life in human form is a window of opportunity, and aging intensifies a sense of urgency. Whatever is going to be done must not be put off. A person nearing the exit of life has a mandate to tell what he knows. David prayed: "Since my youth, O God, You have taught me, and to this day I declare Your marvelous deeds. Even when I am old and gray, do not forsake me, O God, till I declare Your power to the next generation (Ps. 71:17-18, NIV)."

Over and over again (Ps. 102:18; 145:3; Joel 1:3) the theme persists. Psalm 78:2-5 adds a bit of detail: "I will utter things ... we have heard and known, things our fathers have told us.... We will tell the next generation. ... He decreed statutes for Jacob and established the law in Israel, which He commanded our forefathers to teach their children, so the next generation would know them, even the children yet to be born, and they in turn would tell their children" (NIV). The psalm goes on to describe how some who did not know were cowardly in battle. Others are described as stubborn and rebellious. The end result was a life of futility.

Our culture has mislaid the purpose of grandparents. Far more than a pat on the head and expensive gifts is needed. Old people are reservoirs of knowledge and experience, gold deposits waiting to be mined. Almost every family has at least one; we should not let them leave before we invite them lovingly to share and to enrich and to regenerate our own lives.

Ideas for making the most of grandparents:

— Turn on the tape recorder and ask questions (for example, names of family members, poems memorized, memories of school, church, war, the Great Depression, places where you lived)

— Get out old snapshots and trigger some recollections

— Write down recipes and practical how-to's from wise, experienced gray heads

— Go for a drive and focus on nature—stars, animals, birds, flowers, or geological formations.

— Help with a stamp and/or coin collection

— Sing or play music which is meaningful to them

— Celebrate birthdays and anniversaries (be sure to take pictures)

What are the individual needs of the older person? An

overwhelming majority want (or need) to be independent. That is an emotional need, and a very important one. Being swept into the family circle like some overgrown child is humiliating and usually resented by everyone involved. Often when older people are emerging from the grief of the loss of their mate, they do not really know what they want or need. A transitional period is recommended by many geriatric experts.

What are the financial needs? Sometimes monetary help is all that is needed or wanted. I read recently that possibly as many as 4 million older women live on less than $3,000 a year. In my city of Dallas, burglaries, fraud, and purse snatching are the three most often committed crimes against citizens sixty and older. More often the loss is gradual, the quietly increasing gap between income and cost of living. Yet the need often will not be verbalized. The elderly person may be too proud or too embarrassed to ask. Sound financial advice and sensitivity to need is required. Highest respect for the older individual is woven into the scriptural attitude.

What are the health needs? Medical and dental attention need to be made available. Even our government's complex assistance to the elderly in this department recognizes that health considerations are very important. Nearly 1 million people are supported by Medicare in nursing homes and convalescent centers. How much more should families accept this responsibility? Caring is the root attitude.

If an objective and rational decision is mated with an honest and tender concern for the older parent, many problems will be prevented. Nevertheless, circumstances do not always "turn out" as expected. Ill health develops. Loneliness sets in. Interference with young children begins to be resented. Grandma wants to make a temporary arrangement permanent. The "mother-in-law problem," as we call it, has a long gray trail of complaints. Then what?

Some time ago a woman wrote to a syndicated columnist with this problem: her husband had invited his mother to go with them on the first vacation they were having alone since the children grew up. The wife was understandably disappointed, jealous, and resentful. "Mother-in-law problems" appear in many forms. How can one handle them with Christian love?

Middle-aged parents find themselves suspended between two impossibles. On one hand youngsters are rebelling; on the other, aging parents are calling for help. Financially, the middle-aged parents feel anemic from spending. They are trying to parent a younger set who cry, "Let me alone!" and at the same time parent older folks who whine, "You're not going to forget about me, are you?"

At this point principle No. 2, mentioned earlier, comes into play: the husband is the head of the home. He is to "call the shots." It may be difficult for a loving son or son-in-law to stand up and tell an older (and perhaps overbearing) mother that he is in charge. She should respect the son who calmly asserts his headship of the home and who puts his wife first. An older father will also respect the son, because he will identify with him. Most family strife results from blurred roles. We fumble the question: who's in charge here?

Sometimes a family council is necessary. Everybody who lives in a home is concerned with every other one who lives there. When a change is made, all should know about it, and have an opportunity to express an opinion. But the father draws a responsible conclusion.

Domestic difficulties often stem from our insistence on looking at the picture of our homes as an undeveloped negative. We see only the problems in big black blobs. God designed the home for joy, satisfaction, and security. When a home is bathed in the developing solution of God's true intentions, a pleasing picture is the result.

Where but at home can you find a ready-made "fan club" when you are honored, when you achieve?

Where but at home can you be loved for yourself alone, sans shoes, hairdo, and fancy wardrobe?

Where but at home can you talk about the little things that bother you, and get a response that "tells it like it is"?

Where but in the home circle can you shed that specter of loneliness that sooner or later catches up with every unattached person?

God knew exactly what He was doing when He placed Adam in the garden and began home life. Home is the energy source. We all need to be plugged in, like so many appliances, in order to function properly in our individual lives.

*There is no excuse
to huddle in the darkness.
We need to move out
where the action is
and mix it up with
the society to whom
God has called us
to minister.*

THREE
Building a Fire in the Rain

When Joseph arrived in Egypt as a captive of the Ishmaelite traders, he was purchased from them by Potiphar.... Now this man Potiphar was the captain of the king's bodyguard and his chief executioner.... The Lord began blessing Potiphar for Joseph's sake.... Potiphar gave Joseph the complete administrative responsibility over everything he owned.... Joseph, by the way, was a very handsome young man.

One day ... Potiphar's wife began making eyes at Joseph, and suggested that he come and sleep with her. Joseph refused. "Look," he told her, "my master trusts me.... How can I do such a wicked thing as this? It would be a great sin against God."

But she kept on with her suggestions day after day, even though he refused to listen, and kept out of her way as much as possible. Then one day as he was in the house, going about his work—as it happened, no one else was around at the time—she came and grabbed him by the sleeve demanding, "Sleep with me." He tore himself away, but as he did, his jacket slipped off and she was left holding it as he fled from the house. When she saw that she had his jacket, and that he had fled, she began screaming . . . "He tried to rape me, but when I screamed, he ran. . . ."

When her husband came home that night, she told him her story. . . . When her husband heard his wife's story, he was furious. He threw Joseph into prison.　　　　(Excerpted from Genesis 39, TLB)

Here was a man willing to forfeit his freedom in order not to compromise his convictions. May his tribe increase!

In college I had a brilliant, gifted friend who was unreservedly committed to Jesus Christ. In fact, she felt called to the mission field and upon graduation she enrolled in nurses training to prepare for a ministry on foreign soil. She was out of college scarcely six months when she quit. She not only hit bottom, she broke clean through! By her own testimony she will never go to the mission field, never marry. She feels she has disqualified herself on moral grounds.

Not long ago I asked her, "What happened?"

She said, "Howie, as you know, I came from what was called a 'good' Christian home. When I went to nurses training, I discovered it really *wasn't* that good. When the girls would say, 'C'mon, go along with us,' or 'How come you won't do this?' I just didn't have adequate answers. The only thing I could come up with was, 'Because my parents told me not to.' That wears thin!"

My friend's experience forces a question: how can you communicate convictions to your children in such a way that those convictions become not simply secondhand (as with my nurse friend) but their personal property (as with Joseph)?

There are two sides to convictions: negative and positive, the problems and the principles. I would encourage you to sit down together as couples and think through your convictions in terms of what you want to communicate to your children. Let me prime your thinking first with the *problems* you are up against.

The Prevailing Attitude of Passivity
Many parents somehow hope for the best and plod along under the cliché, "We just trust the Lord"—which can be a pitiful cop-out. There's one thing you want to tack in the center of your theological thinking: in both the Old and New Testaments *faith, belief, trust* are *never* passive.

Faith that is genuine is always active. The psalmist put it clearly, "Trust in the Lord and do good" (Ps. 37:3, NASB). You see, your behavior either belies your beliefs or underscores their reality. Are you trusting the Lord for the *means* as well as the *end?* He works in both.

Look at the evidence. Noah sweated through years of preaching, of warning about the flood, of building a boat of radical design. There was no stagnation in Noah's life. He was running a race with a global cloudburst. God said so— and Noah acted.

Abraham put his townhouse up for sale. To settle in the suburbs? Never! He toured the desert like a nomad. He spent a lifetime scouting real estate for his future family. God said, "Move!" Abraham kept moving.

Moses, plucked from the seclusion of the bulrushes, became the favorite of the Egyptian palace. Later, the divine mandate from the burning bush shifted him into high gear. He defied Pharaoh, marched across the Red Sea, wandered through the wilderness, and never stopped until God took him from Mount Nebo—no immobility for Moses.

All of these heroes and many more pleased God because of their faith. The storms of unbelief were raging, but these stalwarts kept on building the fire! There is no excuse for late twentieth-century parents to close their family shutters and huddle in the darkness, just "trusting the Lord." We need to move out where the action is and mix it up with the society to whom God has called us to minister.

The Confusion of Product with Process

We become dreadfully sensitive about the end product because that's what we always see most vividly. The end product is dramatized in the kid who went over the cliff, or off the deep end! You can see the wreckage right in front of your eyes. So it's not hard to discern the product. "Man, I never want that!" you say. But it's not so easy to become sensitized to the process. There is an itinerary, a procedure, a *modus operandi* that eventuated in the end product you observed.

Joseph made a critical—and correct—decision, as cited earlier. Where did he learn his instinctive reactions to immorality? No doubt, many things influenced him, chiefly his own commitment to God. But unfold the early days of Joseph's life and you will see him with his father Jacob. This godly patriarch undoubtedly followed his fatherly duty, as Moses later commanded: "Thou shalt teach them diligently unto thy children, and shalt talk of them when thou sittest in thine house, and when thou walkest by the way, and when thou liest down, and when thou risest up" (Deut. 6:7). Young Joseph had an indelible recording in his mind and heart before his jealous brothers ever threw him into the pit—the first stop on a long and difficult journey. The most adverse circumstances never eroded his convictions.

A Lack of Clear-cut Objectives or Standards

What do you as an individual, or as a couple, *want* for your child? Here's a principle: you can achieve only that for which you aim. If you aim at nothing you will hit it every time. You must have the target clearly in focus. Many people have a very fuzzy idea of what they want to inculcate.

Inconsistency

One real rough spot that manifests itself in at least four areas is inconsistency. First, your standards are *different from the contemporary society* of which you are a part. So, your children are always asking, "Why do *we* do this? How come we're different?"

I remember watching my preschool-age daughter through the window one day. She was on the front driveway counting on her fingers and looking at each home on the street. Pretty soon she came bursting through the door to my wife and asked, "Mommy, why don't you smoke?" She had been out counting all of the women in the neighborhood who smoked. Suddenly she realized her mother was an odd wad. There are many Christian couples who can't choke this down. They are afraid to be different. Distinctively so.

Second, your standards are *different from the Christian community.* My son used to come home and say resentfully, "Daddy, I don't know why *we* can't do it! Dr. _____ lets his kids do it."

Later I'd see that colleague on campus, and I'd say, "Hey, you're a fine friend!"

I'd tell him my story, and he would roar. He'd say, "That's interesting. My boy came home and asked why he couldn't do it. He said Dr. Hendricks lets *his* kids do it!" All of a sudden I got the real picture.

Many of us are patterning our lives after the Christian

community, and the Christian community is going down-hill. The standard of Christian experience is not the Christian community; it's Jesus Christ. If you have to break with the accepted practices of the Christian community to conform yourself to Him, do it.

Cultural or Biblical—Which?

To avoid confusion over the standards of Christians on one hand and Christian standards on the other, tack a little label over these two designations that will help you identify them. The standards of Christians are usually *cultural.* Christian standards are always *biblical.*

I'll never forget being involved in a discussion on a college campus over the issue of hair length for young men. Everybody was so uptight it was unreal. Suddenly the five of us who were talking turned to the wall to see the pictures of the founders of the institution. And thus ended the discussion! You wouldn't believe how much spinach these men had on their heads. They made most of today's young men look like they have crew cuts. What happens in much Christian experience is that we get hung up over something which is culturally oriented and a few years from now will be a dead horse.

Some parents will send a kid to hell for two inches of hair. They make it a federal case! I knew of a Christian couple who chased a son out of their home and told him never to return until he went to a barber shop. He never returned. They're still looking for him—and wishing they had made a better decision. If you're going to take a stand, be sure you take a stand on the crucial issues! Oh, the agony of a father saying, "That's the worst decision I ever made in my life." He knows he acted in the energy of the flesh—certainly not in the power of the Spirit of God—when he sent his boy away.

Third, *your future standards will be different from your present parental convictions.* You have deep-seated convictions? So you think—now. Give yourself ten years and a couple of teenagers, and what you think now are convictions may become unfortunate prejudices. What you thought was relatively trivial suddenly becomes very pivotal, absolutely central. Beware of being insensitive to the Spirit of God, because you ought to be in the process of growing. And so should your convictions!

Fourth, *there is inconsistency because your standards are often different from those of your parents.* There is inherent danger in this. You see, we tend to react against the negatives of our parents while failing to reproduce the positives. I asked a student what turned him off about his parents. He gave me five things—very clearly thought through. "I don't want to produce *that* in my kids!"

"That's good," I agreed. "What *do* you want to produce in your children that your parents produced in you?" Then his thinking was not so clear.

Some of you come from non-Christian homes. Yet even a pagan parent may have communicated significant things to you, because he or she had convictions. Perhaps your parents had nothing to give in the spiritual realm, but they built values into your life that some Christian parents fail to give. Make sure you identify these factors. If you spent the bulk of your teen years dumping disapproval on your parents, then you have a lot of hard, constructive thinking ahead. You have to get rid of the garbage and go back and determine what your parents did that was very good, that you want to reproduce in your children.

Making All the Decisions Ourselves
Too often we are trying to avoid the unpleasant, which is frequently the most profitable from the educational point

of view. There is no growth without tension. A parent's task is to help a child help himself, not to make his decisions for him. You cannot run risks for your children; they must experience them for themselves. I hope you are providing the freedom, the developmental latitude, with which a child can develop into maturity.

Now let's consider some *principles*. Awareness of the problems helps us set our defenses for them; but we must base inculcation of Christian standards on definite principles. Convictions, some people think, are like perfume. You dab some on the warm, pulsating areas of your life, and you hope that your children and those who get close to you will take in the fragrance, enjoy it, and profit by it. But convictions must be made the personal property of each individual. What makes convictions digestible?

Sharpen Your Personal Convictions

Scripture says, "Let every man be fully persuaded in his own mind" (Rom. 14:5). "Be ready always to give an answer" (1 Peter 3:15).

Jeanne tells about her personal confrontation with the principle of honesty. She had been taught to be honest in her Christian home, but that was secondhand truth until one day in a grocery store a clerk gave her too much change. She suffered the temptation, common to many, to keep it and say nothing. The store would never miss it.

In that brief instant, Jeanne became aware that here was the focus of a principle. At that juncture, she made a decision: she vowed to be honest with money, with everything, from there on out. She says that it was a sort of relaxation, no longer a hassle. It required an act of the will; it has become a personal conviction. *Now*, when faced with a decision, she knows what she's going to do *before* a question of honesty arises.

Set Clear Objectives and Priorities

List some things that you definitely want to develop in your family. These may include:

Respect for authority.

Selective friendships.

Learning to take responsibility.

Systematic giving to the Lord.

Obedience. A disciplined walk with the Lord.

A positive self-image.

A responsible use of time.

Giving without expecting a return.

Treating your body as the Lord's.

Looking over this suggested list, I am impressed with what it is going to take to put each item into action. For example, consider respect for authority. This is closely linked with obedience at home. If a child does not learn to obey in the home, he will not learn to obey the law, or civil authority, or the Lord.

You want your child to become a giving person. How giving are *you?* Do you always want your way? Whenever you make a decision as a couple, does your mate always give in to you? The model you provide is the primary means for communicating convictions.

Relationships always precede rules. In fact, they are more important than rules. The principle: a child tends to accept your ideas, your philosophy, because he accepts you. And he tends to reject your ideas and philosophy when he rejects you.

This is interesting to see in terms of a little diagram: Allow the straight line to represent your convictions. You are a parent; God gives you a child. All during childhood, for the most part, he buys your convictions—not that he doesn't question—but generally he conforms. As he moves toward adolescence he veers off. What brings him back?

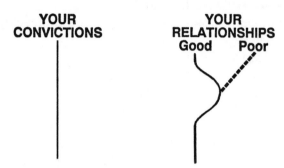

Answer: relationship. What he thinks of you will tend to determine how far back he comes.

The interesting thing is that most children who have a healthy relationship come back, not quite coterminous with their parents, but so close that for all practical purposes they are committed to the same basic things.

If you have a poor relationship, the teen reacts and goes farther away. The more pressure you put on, the farther out he goes—to prove that he is quite independent of you. If you have a good relationship with a child he never has to prove anything.

Let Love Be Supreme
Without love, the child reacts rather than acts. Deprivations of loving discipline in childhood leave deep scars of pathological anxiety—even if he has received spiritual and moral teaching.

This lack is my explanation for why many kids reared in Christian homes kick over the traces. The home did not lack clear-cut moral teaching, but the moral teaching took place in a context lacking meaningful love (in which the parent does that which is best for the child).

Love always acts in the child's best interests, even if the child does not understand at that particular point in time.

You are not interested in how he feels and reacts now as much as how he feels and reacts ten to fifteen years from now. True love treats the child now in terms of the future. "Now" love should be alive with activity.

The reverberations of this home energy can be felt in Norman Corwin's graphic description of the components of home life: "Of course a home without love is just cold real estate . . . [it] is a minuscule world. If it has ten books, it is partly a library; if three pictures, a little museum; if six tools, a repair shop; if one big, crowded closet of bric-a-brac, a warehouse. Whenever a piano or fiddle is in serious use, it is a part-time conservatory. At mealtime grace, or in answering a child's question about God, it is a fraction of a church. In the throes of argument or the heat of discourse, it becomes a court; in sickness it is a field hospital; when you discover old forgotten letters, pictures, souvenirs in a trunk or attic, it is a wing of archaeology. When the kids climb trees, fences, high furniture, or other forbidden obstacles, it is a commando camp . . ." (*Reader's Digest*).

Explain Your Convictions

"The father to the children shall make known Thy truth" (Isa. 38:19). In order to explain our convictions we must have communication, but sometimes the lines are frozen. On Thanksgiving Day, a young mother was seated in the den of her home with a group of friends and relatives. Her six-year-old daughter came in and whispered in her ear, "Mommy, I need to tell you something."

"OK, Honey, tell me."

"I can't tell you *here*," she whispered frantically.

"Oh, yes, you can, just say it out loud."

"No, Mommy, I can't."

And that was the end of the dialogue.

Three or four days later, the young woman heard (from a

friend in whose home her daughter had visited) of an incident that had taken place involving moral implications. "Your daughter was pretty upset," the friend told her.

Later, when the woman asked her daughter why she hadn't told her about the incident, the little girl responded, "Mommy, I *tried* to, but you wouldn't listen, and Uncle Jack was sitting there, and I couldn't say it in front of him!" That mother learned a hard lesson—she lost a choice opportunity for communicating. "From here on out," she said, "when my child is ready to talk, I'm ready to listen."

Listening and answering. It's the open communication line at the vital moment. Moses knew about explaining to children. He counseled the Israelite parents, "In the years to come, when your son asks you, 'What is the purpose of these laws which the Lord our God has given us?' you must tell him" (Deut. 6:20, TLB).

Live Your Convictions Consistently

Children are not looking for perfect parents, but they are looking for honest parents. An honest, progressing parent is a highly infectious person. Your convictions are much more caught than taught. A child unconsciously patterns his life after a model in his environment. Unfortunately, many children do not have adequate models. I believe the primary problem with rebellious teens is the lack of reliable models.

Dr. Albert Bandura of Stanford University, a man who has done more research in the modeling field than perhaps anyone, made this statement: "In our research at Stanford University we have found that any learning outcome that results from direct experience can also come about on a vicarious basis through observation of other people's behavior and its consequences for them."

When a child watches you in the process of growth,

she watches Jesus Christ being formed in you; that is a highly commendable thing to her. Ask yourself: "What is there in my life that I cannot account for on any other basis than the supernatural?"

Dr. Thomas Harris, a twenty-five-year veteran of psychiatric practice, in his best-selling book, *I'm OK—You're OK*, warns against inconsistency in parents of small children. "When they say 'don't lie,' and then the child hears them lying, this produces confusion and fear, and the child tries to tune out the discordance." Harris illustrates the principle with an algebraic equation: "A plus times a minus equals a minus. It does not matter how big the plus was, or how little the minus was. The result is always a minus. . . . The effects in later life may be ambivalence, discord, and despair." Christian parents need to be certain that what they say and what they do harmonizes.

Feed Your Children Responsibility

You don't become a responsible person overnight; it requires a process. Feeding responsibility is risky. It means we have to allow children to do some things that we would probably rather do for them. We give them the privilege of exercising their own free will. As a result there are going to be some casualties along the way. Sometimes they are going to fall—where you think they shouldn't fall.

My son Bill was at a California camp while I was fulfilling a speaking engagement nearby. He came running to where we were staying and said, "I don't wanna stay there." We encouraged him to go back, but three times he came, complaining. Each time we gently returned him with cheerful assurances, not wanting him to succumb to weakness.

The third time, however, we also inquired from his counselor if anything could be done. We learned that his cabinmates were making fun of his Texas accent. The camp director made some changes, and the week ended successfully, with our boy wanting to stay when it came time to leave. He learned to accept this responsibility of being away from his parents, but he learned it little by little. Constantly pushing them out—gently forcing them to be responsible for themselves—builds self-confidence.

Responsibility is developed over a lifetime. We are all in the process of developing. Give your children the privilege of an early start, so that when they step out of home, they have a background of living with their own decisions.

Sometimes the biggest hang-up of all is letting the child go. It stabs us. "He's going away," we sob. It's really not so big a hassle with the child as with the parents.

Houseclean Your Attitudes

Atmosphere and climate are paramount in communicating convictions. I would suggest that the most important thing you contribute to a child is to allow him the luxury of a mistake. Let him know he is free to fail.

Do you refuse to look failure in the face? Do you overlook the benefits that are implicit in a mistake? Jesus Christ allowed His men to fail in order to learn. He let Peter sink into the water—to train him to keep his eyes on Christ (Matt. 14:28-31). He allowed His disciples to fail in their attempt at casting out a demon—to learn the weakness of the flesh (Matt. 17:14-21). Failure has a rightful place in the Christian home. It is sometimes necessary to lose minor skirmishes in order to win a lifetime struggle.

Share personal failures. It is a great encouragement to children to know that Mom and Dad failed sometimes too. On one occasion we were discussing our witness for Christ. My wife related her failure to buy up several opportunities which the Lord had given her to inquire into a young student's spiritual welfare. She had known him as a classmate, a debate team member, and she had flown on the same plane with him and chatted in the Los Angeles airport. She saw him again on a Honolulu-bound jet. The last time she saw him, he was reeling into a bar in Waikiki. Two months later she learned that he had been killed in a train wreck in Africa during a trip around the world! She had talked with him at the beginning of the trip but never shared her faith. This sad failure was described to our children to emphasize the importance of buying up opportunities. It was, undoubtedly, an encouragement to them to know that their parents sometimes strike out too.

Seek God's Will, Not Your Own
Getting a child to conform to the will of the Lord is probably the ultimate goal of all Christian parents who have themselves experienced the pleasure and satisfaction and fulfillment of living in God's will. Reiterate to your children: "It is not so important how you relate to us, as how you relate to Christ." As our children have grown older, this has taken on new meaning for them.

When they are young, they follow their parents. Paul wrote, "Follow *me* as I follow Christ." Our first principle was "sharpen your personal convictions." Your children will imitate you as the beginning of the process which leads to imitation of Christ. All along the way we parents must set the example of relating to Christ. This underscores the tremendous responsibility of parenthood concerning one's own personal life.

We want our children to follow a person, not a set of rules. We must recognize that as maturity increases, the need for rules decreases. Let me illustrate it this way: You want to learn typing. You enroll in a course and are placed in a room full of typewriters. You look at the keys and every one of them is blank! How will you ever learn to operate the thing—there are no labels on it!

Then you receive a book with a picture of the keyboard. In learning to type, you don't look at the typewriter, but at the printed keyboard—the picture, the chart. It would be utterly useless to manipulate the chart; it has no power of itself. But by reading the chart, by having it make an indelible impression on your mind, you become capable of using the keyboard. You can then take away the chart and type without any letters on the keys.

In somewhat the same way, we parents are to be the picture and chart that our children look at when they are young. Even as one learns to use a typewriter by using a chart, the children will learn to trust Christ by looking at the parental model, and then in their mature years relate to Jesus Christ on their own.

Simple authority in the home no longer awes them. It is not enough that the parent should know something. To establish credentials to be heard, the parent must also be someone who in some personal or moral way merits their attention. Children seem to be saying not "What do you know?" but "Who are you and what do you believe in that merits our attention?"

Which would you rather have your son become: a garbage collector or a missionary? That really depends on the will of God. I would rather have my son a garbage collector in the will of God than a missionary out of the will of God.

One day your child says, "Dad, I want to be a missionary."

"Wonderful!" you say and you never let him forget it.

But one day the little toddler is in the backyard and as the trash is collected, he comes running in. "Mommy, I wanna be a garbageman." You laugh, and you never remind him of that. Why not?

What do you really want your child to be? Is it something that will reflect most favorably on you? Or is it something that will reflect most favorably on Jesus Christ?

Inculcating Christian standards is like building a fire in the rain. It requires willful determination, against all odds, to do what seems impossible. It calls for expertise—know-how which understands the nature of the child and the nature of a hostile world. It demands a stubborn perseverance to keep fanning the flickering flame, to keep protecting the hot coals. A warm young life, glowing for Christ, is the most needed commodity in the damp, depressing chill of the marketplace today.

*Every good parent
practices two forms
of discipline—
corrective and
preventive discipline.*

FOUR

Your Rod—a Serpent or a Staff?

Humpty Dumpty sat on a wall;
Humpty Dumpty had a great fall.
All the king's horses and all the king's men
Couldn't put Humpty together again.

What a perceptive parable of our time! We are living in a generation in which everything nailed down is coming loose. The things that people once said could not happen *are* happening. And thoughtful, though often unregenerate, individuals are asking, "Where is the glue with which to reassemble the disintegrating and disarrayed parts?"

Nowhere is this disintegration more clearly seen than in the realm of authority. Whether governmental, societal, or parental, discipline is declining.

It's a manifest fact that we are creatures of extremes. Invariably we suffer from the peril of the pendulum. Too many parents assume the role of a Simon Legree. They nail the kid to the floor every time he squeaks; they make a federal case out of every misdemeanor. Others become overly permissive, paralyzed by their child's behavior, scared to death to lay a hand on him for fear of permanently damaging his psyche.

If Junior decides to throw a brick through a plate glass window, don't stop him. After all, you are likely to curb his genius for throwing bricks!

In the midst of the reality of home life we need an authoritative base for daily disciplinary decisions. Let's examine a slice of Scripture that sets forth a foundation.

The Revelation of Christian Discipline

The last three chapters of Ephesians are a patrol guide: how to walk by faith when there's a war on. Paul underscores a series of family relationships, and one is the relationship or responsibility of parents to children.

Ephesians 6:4 states: "And, you fathers, stop provoking your children to anger, but bring them up in the chastening and instruction of the Lord" (author's translation).

Mark it well; this command is addressed to fathers, not because discipline is their exclusive role, but because it is their established (and exacting) responsibility. Gentlemen, you can never palm this off on your wife. If your children are not disciplined, that is *your* problem. God is holding *you* responsible.

This does not mean that the father is to do all the disciplining, as suggested by, "You just wait till your father comes home!" But father is *responsible* for all that is done—or not done. The father, as the head of that home, is the one, under God, who will have to give an account of his stewardship. He will never be able to say, as Adam did, "The woman whom Thou gavest to be with me" (see Gen. 3:12).

"Provoke not your children to wrath" (Eph. 6:4). This is a very intriguing expression in the original Greek text. It can be translated one of two ways. Either Paul is saying, "Stop provoking your children to anger," or he could be saying, "Don't get the habit of provoking your children." If you're doing it, cut it out! If you're not doing it, don't ever start!

Frequently, people ask, "How does one provoke children to anger?" The answer is by either overdisciplining or underdisciplining. Interestingly enough, both extremes produce the same result—insecurity.

Children need corrective discipline. Is it essential? Absolutely. Someone asked evangelist Grady Wilson on one occasion, "Did your mother ever spank you?"

"Did she ever spank me? She had a strap in the kitchen which hung under the motto, 'I need thee every hour!' "

That's *corrective* discipline.

Unfortunately, too many parents know only this form of discipline. I was riding in a police car one night when we picked up a kid who had been beaten into unconsciousness by his father. The officer and I counted sixty-seven major welts on this boy's body. When we contacted his father, the first thing he wanted to assure us was that he was a disciplinarian. The truth is, he didn't know anything about discipline. There are too many people running around with a biblical two-by-four who really don't know very much of what the Scriptures teach regarding discipline.

"Cut it out!" "Shut up!" "Stop it!" The kid is seven before he learns his name is not Shut Up! It's amazing how much of this goes under the name of Christian teaching. Often it is really some parent venting his or her spleen!

As previously mentioned, Paul offers a workable option: "Bring them up by *chastening* and *instruction.*"

Every competent physician practices two forms of medicine: corrective medicine and preventive medicine. Every good parent practices two forms of discipline—corrective and preventive. Unfortunately, too many of us define discipline only in its corrective aspect.

Corrective discipline always has a context. It is reinforced and made workable by preventive discipline. The effectiveness of corrective discipline is always determined by the relationship you build in preventive discipline. For example, I ask, "Do you play with your child?" If you don't play with him, you have no right to spank him.

"Oh," you say, "I'm his parent; I can do anything I want."

That's right, but you cannot guarantee the results.

Do you listen to your child? I did not ask if you talk to him; I know the answer to that! When was the last time you threw yourself across your daughter's bed and said, "Honey, tell me what happened today. I'd like to hear ..." and then listened with real interest and personal attachment?

Do you spend time with your children? Do you know the joy of informal rap sessions with your teens? Perhaps you're sitting in your robe and kids are sprawled on the floor—just talking—and you're listening, captivated and involved.

Or are you a sermon-preacher at home (preaching without a license!)? "Now it is time for Dad (or Mom) to talk!" You cannot program adolescents. You listen when they *want* to talk. Sometimes until the wee hours of the morning. That may be the time you get through to them. It's not the quantity of time; it's the quality of the relationship that cuts it! It's not how much but what kind.

Some parents are prone to get all shook up over reading a chapter like this. "OK, Jimmy, c'mon, we're gonna play. The book says I'm supposed to play with you. I don't have a lot of time. C'mon, let's go—get the ball." You heave the ball with resentment right into his middle. What you are really telling him is that there are 100 other places you'd rather be than playing with him—and you might as well be at any one of the 100.

How much better to say, "Hey, Buddy, I only have ten minutes, but there's nothing I'd rather do than spend it with you! What would you like to do? Play ball?" You go out and throw the ball around, look at your watch, and say, "Wow! that was the fastest ten minutes I spent today. We'll have to do this more often."

The curious result is that the child has more insight than you do. What really tears a kid up is not that you don't have more time, but what you choose to do when you *do* have time. Do you make the decision, "I want to spend my time with you"?

Some years ago I was on the grass wrestling with my son, Bill. We had been dislodged from the living room, where it all began. My wife is unusual—she doesn't appreciate a heated wrestling match in the living room—imagine that! My boy got me in a hold, and I wanted to teach him how to break it. So I pivoted. Unfortunately, I got too much leverage and he went flying through the air like a missile. "Good night! He's going to have a concussion! They'll try me for child abuse!" I cringed inside.

Bill bounced on the unyielding ground, jumped up, and squealed, "Boy, Dad, that was terrific! Do it again!"

Now the same child would have dissolved in tears if I had spanked him lightly on the bottom. What's the difference? It's all a matter of relationship—relationships determine response. It's not the physical force, but the personal friendship. "The dad who corrects me is also the dad who wrestles with me," concludes the child. Do you fix his bicycle tire or her doll house? One message confirms the other. The hardest thing for a child to resist is the displeasure of a parent who has built a strong relationship with him.

The Requisites of Christian Discipline
Now let's take God's truth and relate it to our experience.

There are two words I am always careful never to use—
those words are "always" and "never." Let me suggest
some things you ought always never use.

1. Don't use comparisons of one child with another.
"Kimberly, why aren't you good like Jennifer?" One intelligent answer: "I'm not Jennifer." (Besides, it's most unbibli-
cal to teach your child to keep his eyes on another
person—that can be lethal!)

My wife and I have four children. We never cease to be
amazed at how different they are—even though they are
the products of the same home and parents. If I said, "Is
that the best you can do?" to a certain one of my children,
he'd come right up out of the rocks and respond beautifully. If I said the same thing to another, a better job would
probably be the last thing he would do.

We are always looking for the parental pharmacist with
the patent medicine approach: what are the things you
always do under *every* circumstance to *always* get guaranteed results? There is no such medicine. This may be one
reason God gives most of us more than one child. He wants
us to recognize they are individual persons, not products.

2. Don't make fun of a child—especially of his weak-
nesses. The male of the species is a master with the needle.
He may even have practiced before the children were
born—on Mom. Coming home from the office, he is heard
to bellow, "Well, dear, what's the burnt offering for supper
tonight?" That really produces a Betty Crocker every time!
Sarcasm is like sulfuric acid to human relationships.

I have seen a child with a mild speech problem—occa-
sional stuttering—develop a severe disability because a
Ph.D. father and a highly educated mother mimicked their
son every time he stuttered. His parents had the dubious
distinction of permanently handicapping this young man.

It is relatively easy to recognize such failure in its extreme forms. What you may fail to see is what you are doing every day to develop noncorrectable patterns in your own child. Are you on your child's back or on her team? Get off her back; get on her team.

Be available—attend the games, the concerts, the science fairs, the drama productions, the PTA. Wear your parent badge with pride. It takes more than words to say: "I am honored to be identified with you." That kind of support enriches the soil in which self-esteem grows best.

3. Don't use idle threats or bribes. I was being entertained in a home where a very bright-eyed grade-schooler was sitting across the dinner table from me. Her mother gave her a helping of mashed potatoes. Then a process unfolded that I have termed "operation rhubarb."

"Sally, eat your mashed potatoes" (in proper parental tone).

"Sally, would you please eat your mashed potatoes for Mommy?" (more plaintive)

"Sally! Eat your mashed potatoes!" (shouting)

"Sally, if you don't eat your mashed potatoes you won't get any dessert" (a soft, slow burn).

I couldn't take my eyes off Sally. She winked at me. Sure enough, soon Mother removed the mashed potatoes and brought Sally a huge portion of ice cream. I thought, "Sally is smarter than her mother. She is a better student of her mother than her mother is of her." It was a case of "Parents, obey your children," rather than, as the Bible says, "Children, obey your parents."

Avoid bribes—they'll get you over a barrel. "Son, if you keep quiet in church today, Daddy will buy you that bat you want." Dad thinks he's solving the problem. Actually, he's creating a greater one. All true discipline has as its goal self-discipline, the development of internal controls.

4. Don't be afraid to say no. Many parents with whom I

have counseled confess that they were afraid to carry out what they knew was best for the child. I ask, "Afraid? Of what?"

The usual response is, "I feared my child would turn against me, that he would think I didn't love him."

You will seldom lose a child by doing the right thing for him. Intelligent, scriptural love is always unconditional. You may not like what your child does, but you always love him no matter what his response is.

What Will He Think of You When He's Grown?

If you love your child, you will provide discipline. If you do not discipline, you do not really love.

You cannot evaluate discipline on the basis of what your child in his immaturity thinks about what you are doing. Your primary concern is not what he thinks of you now, but what he will think twenty years from now.

We once had a seminary student from New York—twenty-four years of age and he had never once been away from home. His mother took him to college in New York every day and picked him up. Then God called him to the ministry, and to train—of all places—at Dallas. That's a long way from New York. So she bought him an American Airlines ticket, put him on an American Airlines plane, fastened his American Airlines seat belt, and sent him to us.

When he arrived he was the sickest puppy you've ever seen. "I'm homesick," he told me.

"I can appreciate that, my friend," I replied, "but it looks like you have a great laboratory in which to work this thing out—for four years."

He went to see various professors, and one of them was discussing him with me as I left on Friday for a weekend of ministry. "You'd better keep your eye on him," I said, "because I think he's going home." Monday morning I got the word—he had gone home. His mother had wired him the money to buy the homebound ticket. Doesn't that really seem sad?

Later we got the sequel to the story. This young man was drafted into the Army. And he *couldn't* go home! Probably the best thing that happened to him. The point is: anytime you do something for your child that your child is capable of doing for himself, you are building an emotional cripple.

Let's look at the *positive* side. What should we do?

1. *Impart the expectancy of obedience.* Some parents never expect their children to obey and thus they are seldom disappointed.

My son was playing with a friend outside my study window. I heard this high-pitched call: "Johnny!"

Johnny never flinched.

My boy said, "Johnny, your mother's calling you" (as if he needed the information!).

"Yeah, I know," Johnny said, totally ignoring her.

This went on for four or five times, each time the decibel level rising considerably. Finally she exploded with an intensely shrill scream, "Johnny!"

As calmly as can be, Johnny said to my son, "Bill, I gotta go now." Johnny had been down that road before and he knew exactly when his mother meant what she said.

I had to visit in the home of a fourteen-year-old delinquent boy once. There was no bell to ring, so I knocked on the screen door and the young fellow responded. He recognized me and invited me to come in and have a seat. Then he said, "I bet you're thirsty, aren't you, Mister." It was a hot day and I was. "I'll go get you some water." He disappeared into the kitchen and came back with a peanut butter jar, not too well washed, filled with water.

Just about the time he got to me, his mother appeared in the door. "Get outa here!" she screamed, and he dumped the whole thing right down the front of me. I have rarely heard a woman—or a man—curse as she did. "That kid can't do anything right!"

"You know, Lady," I replied, "I hate to start this interview on a negative note, but I couldn't disagree with you more. I'm proud of your boy."

"Whad'ya mean, you're proud of him? Look at what he did to *you.*"

"Did you ever make a mistake?" I asked. "To be perfectly honest, if you had shouted at me the way you did at him I'd have spilled that water too."

"He can't do anything right," she repeated again.

"Lady, as long as you continue to say 'he can't,' he won't."

Do you ever tell your child he can't? Telling a child he can't is the basic building block for the shaky structure of inferiority feelings. One of my primary tasks as a professor in an evangelical theological seminary is to come across to students who perhaps for the first time have found somebody who believes in them. I hope, by God's grace, you believe in your child, that you are on his team.

2. *Don't be afraid to admit your mistakes.* I arrived home around 8 o'clock one night after a long day of teaching at the seminary. As I walked in the front door, I encountered a clear case of attempted homicide. My two boys were at it again. So I moved into action and disciplined the older boy (obviously the aggressor). As I went into the bedroom my lovely wife said, "Sweetheart, you missed."

"How's that?"

"Let me tell you what happened *before* you arrived."

Of course, her explanation completely changed the picture, and I had to do what I think is very difficult for any parent—apologize. I went out to the kitchen where the older boy, still sobbing, had been assigned to the dishpan. I said, "Bob, I'm very sorry; I acted too soon; I goofed. I didn't have all the facts." I'll never forget his putting his arm around me and saying, "Sure, Dad, that's OK. We all make mistakes."

We sure do—even parents (and seminary professors!). Your child does not expect you to be a perfect parent, but he does expect you to be an honest one—secure enough to say, "I made a mistake."

3. *Allow the child to express his or her own viewpoint.* My students asked me to make a tape of one of our family councils when the children were quite small. We happened to be discussing the problem of tidiness. I realize this is not a hassle for many, but there are times when our house seems to resemble a tornado alley!

In the course of the discussion, my children were all confessing the sins of their sister, Beverly, who at the time was about four years old.

Little Bev jarred the symposium with a broadside: "But, Daddy, you didn't lower it!"

Do you know what she was talking about? Do you have closets in your home? Check out how high the clothes rod is—especially in terms of a four-year-old. I had promised, "Honey, one of these days Daddy will lower it so you can hang up your clothes." But I had not done so.

You see, we were expecting a child of four to do something that was absolutely impossible for her to do. Furthermore, we made no provision to help.

Childishness or Rebellion? There's a Difference
Much discipline is arbitrary and without value, because it presupposes a maturity the child does not possess. There is an important distinction between childishness and rebellion. Don't confuse them.

A Dallas woman, mother of three girls, shared a quotation with one of my classes that impressed me as loaded with realism. She had been struck by the sobering responsibility of having a teenager. One day she told her oldest daughter, "Darling, I just want you to know I've never been down this road before. You're the first teen I've ever had, and I'm sure I'm going to make some mistakes. But I want you to know that I love you, and everything I do will be because I love you. If I discover I'm wrong, I'll be the first one to tell you." You never get a negative reaction from an approach like that.

4. *Remember that discipline is a long-range process.*

When my wife and I were married we were given a lovely set of pottery. In time our children arrived and we faced a critical decision. Will we keep the dishes intact and have children who do not know how to wash and dry dishes? Or will we train the children to do the dishes, and perhaps in the process lose a few? If you want to know which route we took, you should see the one remaining remnant in our china closet!

Allow your children the luxury of a few mistakes. There is something worse—not making mistakes and arresting growth. Maturity comes with responsibility.

When I was a boy, I loved to play checkers. In fact, I fashioned myself to be something of a champion checker player. There was an elderly gentleman in the community who was purported to be the best, but in my naïveté, I felt the reason he had that reputation was that he had never played me.

One day I was hanging around when the action was not too heavy where he played. To my surprise, he said, "Son, how would you like to play checkers?" Before he finished getting the words out, I was busy setting up the checkers on the board.

We exchanged a few moves, and then he fed me a checker and said, "Jump me." And then another, and another. I thought, "This is easier than I expected!"

As if it were yesterday, I can still remember the puff of his pipe and the wry smile which broke out on his lips as I watched him take a checker and move through my men to the other side—"King me!" Would you believe, he wiped every checker I had off the board with one king, and I got a liberal arts education concerning playing checkers. No good checker player minds losing a few checkers—as long as he's headed for king territory.

Did you, as a parent, lose a few checkers this week? The question is, where are you headed? King territory? Do you see your child as a problem or a potential? Do you see him in terms of what he is or in terms of what he is to become by the power of God working in him—and in you?

To the believer,
worship is not
a luxury;
it is life.

FIVE
Heaven-to-Home Hotline

One of the most remarkable revelations of God to be found in His Word is that which portrays Him as the seeking God. For example, in Luke 19:10 we read, "For the Son of man is come to seek and to save that which was lost." God in quest of souls to save—that is the genius of the Gospel. That is why Christianity is *not* a religion. All religions have one thing in common—they are man's search for God. Christianity is a revelation—of God's search for man. It was God who came walking in the cool of the garden asking, "Adam, where are you?"

John 4 reveals something amazing about the seeking God through the record of our Saviour's encounter with the woman of Samaria. She sought to embroil Him in a discussion concerning the location of worship. Our Lord put His finger on the real issue: "Ye worship ye know not what; we know what we worship, for salvation is of the Jews. But the hour cometh, and now is, when the true worshipers shall worship the Father in spirit and in truth; *for the Father seeketh such to worship Him*" (v. 22). Don't ask me to explain that last phrase; I can't. I'm only thankful to God that I can experience it. I've never recovered from the impact of this truth: God is seeking *my* worship. We grieve the Holy Spirit when we spurn that which He seeks.

A student came into my office and said, "Prof, I'm not getting very much out of my quiet time." I'm sure I jarred him no end when I said, "My friend, did it ever occur to you that it really makes very little difference what you get out of it? The important thing is what God gets out of it, and God is seeking your worship."

To the believer, worship is not a luxury; it is life. It's not optional; it's essential. It's not something reserved for a body of individuals who might engage in it if and when they have the time and concern. It is the Christian's highest occupation.

Worship is a personal response to divine revelation. God has revealed Himself, and it is up to me to respond. But, alas, worship is the lost chord of evangelicalism. It's largely missing in our churches. But worse—and probably the reason it's missing at church—worship is gone from our homes.

Let's examine the excuses often pawned öff as reasons for not having family worship.

"I Don't Have Time"
Having time for family worship is a matter of priorities. You don't have time for what? To do that which God is seeking?

I was pastoring in the city of Fort Worth, Texas. A father of five there was very remiss in his attendance at the Sunday worship services and extremely delinquent as a father. He was the object of my concern, and I paid a pastoral call to confront him with his defection. In the course of the conversation he said, "Pastor, you don't understand. I don't have time; I gotta work."

"Who said you had to work?" I asked.

"It's obvious," he replied. "If you don't work you don't eat."

"Who said you had to eat?" I persisted.

"Oh, c'mon, Pastor," he said. "Be realistic. If you don't eat, you don't live!"

"Well, who said you have to live?" I asked. "Give me one verse of Scripture that says you have to live. Did it ever occur to you that it would be better for you to die in fellowship with Jesus Christ than to go on living outside of fellowship with Him?"

"I never thought of it that way," he said. (I hadn't either, but I didn't tell him that!)

But this is the issue: how high on your priority list is fellowship with the infinite God?

Mark 1:35 is an insightful verse of Scripture: "In the morning, rising up a great while before day, He went out and departed into a solitary place and there prayed." What morning? Why, the morning after the busiest recorded day in the life of our Lord Jesus. Only fifty-two days of Christ's life on earth are recorded in the Gospels. Chapter 1 of Mark records a very busy day, a day crowded with performing miracles, with teaching, with exposure to people. Only a person who has had exposure to large groups of people can appreciate the drain of such a day upon the individual. And in the morning—after that busy day—He arose before dawn to have fellowship with His Father. That's how high it was on His priority list.

Have you learned anything about the barrenness of busyness? We are living in an activistic society, which, unfortunately, has rubbed off on us. There can be a sterility to activity. Much of it is nothing more than an anesthetic to deaden the pain of an empty life.

"It's Inconvenient"

The average person is looking for a religion that is comfortable and convenient. And there are plenty of them on the market. But you cannot take cost and conflict out of Christianity and still have the genuine item.

I can say very emphatically from experience, if you are looking for a convenient time to have family worship, forget it. It will never be easy. In fact, I am convinced that the devil will cut loose with everything in his arsenal to bomb out your family worship—anything to keep you from fellowship with the Father.

A verse in 2 Samuel 24 gives a glimpse into the life of David. "Neither will I offer burnt offerings unto the Lord my God of that which doth cost me nothing" (v. 24). You see, there is a price tag to worshiping the living God. It costs you nothing to accept the gift of God which is eternal life. It may cost you everything for a spiritual life with virility and impact.

"Keep thy heart with all diligence," warns Proverbs 4:23, "for out of it are the issues of life." The Christian life is a discipline, not a dream.

"I Don't Know How"

The matter of technique is probably the most legitimate problem Christians have regarding family worship. Maybe you didn't come from a Christian home and have no model. This was my problem. When I recognized my responsibility, I was like a babe in the woods.

Some years ago I was ministering at Mount Hermon and in the course of a message mentioned the family altar. At the end of the session a lady came forward and asked, "About that family altar, do they handle them here in the bookstore?" I engaged her in conversation and discovered she was from a Catholic background, and I understood immediately. You can go to a Roman Catholic bookstore and get a little set of equipment and you're in business. Now that she had become an evangelical, she thought there must be a similar set of equipment.

I can sympathize with this woman, because I find that those of us in the preaching/teaching field are often long on exhortation but short on explanation. We are constantly telling people *what* they ought to do but we don't often bother to tell them *how*.

"I Don't Need It"

A man said to me, "You're going overboard on this family worship thing. Isn't it enough to go to church on Sunday?" This is compartmentalized Christianity—the little religious routine on Sunday with the Lord on call the rest of the week in case of trouble.

But the Bible says, "Whatsoever ye do in word or deed, do all in the name of the Lord Jesus, giving thanks to God and the Father by Him" (Col. 3:17). Christianity affects all of life. It revolutionizes the whole of human experience.

Excuses evaporate upon examination. There's quite a difference between a good sound reason and a reason that sounds good. If you want to have family worship, you will find a way. If you don't, you will find an excuse.

What goes into a stimulating family worship experience?

Learn to Talk to God

Family worship should include a time when you talk to God. Early in our own family life, we used a loose-leaf notebook. On one side was written, "We Ask," and on the other side, "He Answers." I wouldn't exchange for anything what this taught my children about the theology of prayer. There is nothing quite so instructive to a child as writing down something specific for which he asks God, then, as

God responds to his faith, experiencing the excitement and enthusiasm—and instruction—of writing "yes" on the answer side of the page.

There are times when we have had to write "no." Have you reminisced over the unwise requests you made of God? He said no. A good father does not grant every wish. He gives only what is best.

Timing is often very important. Sometimes God answers prayer with "wait." Not because God isn't ready, but often because we are not ready.

I hope it doesn't disturb you that your children pray for the bicycle, the dog, the fence, the sandpile, and all the other realities in their young lives.

I had a man in my home a number of years ago who was a scholar. The reason I know is that he told me so three times! He participated in our time of family worship. In typical style our children prayed for the fence, and thanked the Lord for the tricycle. I could tell this was rotting his theological socks. Afterward he took me aside and said, "Professor Hendricks, you don't mean to tell me you teach at a theological seminary and you encourage your children to pray about things like that!"

"Certainly! Do you ever pray for your Ford?" I knew he did; he was riding mostly on faith and fabric.

He answered, "Oh, yes, of course."

I responded, "Whatever made you think your Ford is more important to God than my boy's tricycle?" I pressed that home.

"Do you ever pray for protection?" I asked.

He said, "Oh, I never get into my car but what I pray about the hazards of the highway."

I explained, "Protection is what my girl is praying for when she thanks Jesus for the fence that keeps out those great big dogs!"

The problem of becoming an adult is that you get educated beyond your intelligence! A child needs to pray at the level of his own understanding and needs.

Learn to Listen to God

In prayer, we talk to the Lord; but in the Bible, God talks to us. One principle is paramount. Don't multiply Scripture; make it meaningful. There is nothing magical about reading 417 verses. Spirituality is not determined by how much of the Bible you read each day. The constant feedback we get from grown young people is, "Family worship was so boring!" You know, Mom takes her tour of the mission field; Dad reviews his theology. It's really a bad scene!

My wife and I visited a family in Holland. The children spoke no English; yet they communicated well to us. After dinner we shared their family worship time. There were three children: a preschooler, a first-grader, and a third-grader. Along with their mother, they pantomimed Scripture for us. We were told to watch carefully because we would have to interpret what they were acting out, and no words would be spoken.

We witnessed a portrayal of the Parable of the Lost Sheep. Next they did Esther before Ashasuerus—that was a rough one! Finally, they acted out the episode of Paul's imprisonment, with his nephew informing the authorities. You can imagine how long all of this was. We had to watch carefully. The impact that came through to us was how well they knew the details of the stories and were able to project the ideas to us without words. Best of all, every one of us enjoyed the experience.

It doesn't have to be boring to be biblical! It's a crime to bore a person with the Word of God. Bore him with Emerson or Shakespeare or nuclear physics, but not with the Bible! Use modern translations and paraphrases to transfer

God's Word into words your children and teens can digest and absorb—their heart language!

Get It All Together

What constitutes a meaningful worship time in the home? Let me give you some of the characteristics:

Timing is not important, but regularity is. Morning? Evening? It depends on your family. The important thing is to find a time when you can get all the family together—a time you can keep.

Try to be brief, but not rushed. Some people think to have something holy it must be at least an hour or more. That is not true.

Keep it varied. Obviously variety demands creative planning. In talking with seminary students who have come from Christian homes, I have discovered the one thing they resented about a family worship time is that it was so dull—always the same.

Plan a different theme and prayer subject for each day. For example, Monday is ready-made for a review of what you learned in church the day before. Pray specifically for your witness in the community, and in the schools and businesses where family members are involved.

Two days a week can be devoted to missionaries. Read missionary stories in serial fashion. Correspond with your missionaries by tape and letter. There is a little part of Africa closer to us than some parts of Dallas because we as a family made the needs of a Bible school there our personal family concern.

Another day pray for relatives. Those close to us and related by blood are often the most difficult ones with whom to share our faith. We need supernatural help to win our relatives to Jesus Christ.

Review memory work. Pray for family problems, goals,

and needs, for your pastor and local church needs. Use special occasions and holidays for a unique worship focus, related to the theme of the season.

As the children grow, allow them freedom in helping to plan and to participate. It *is* family worship, not parent worship. Remember especially thanksgiving. Build a sense of gratitude with frequent reinforcement of the truth of God's goodness in our lives.

Another component in family worship is music. A great tragedy of the day is that our children are not reared knowing the hymns of the faith. We took it as a project in our family to learn some of the hymns. They are easily remembered—food that sticks to the spiritual ribs.

Devotional materials are also a component. At the end of this chapter is a list of suggested resources which have proved useful in enlivening many a family worship session. Try them—you'll like them!

Don't be afraid to be original. Use tapes, videos, art and craft projects, drama, puppets—all these teaching tools and more are available to draw a family together in worship.

Also, the sessions should be *informal.* One doesn't have to be preachy. Keep things primarily child-centered. Every one of the children who is old enough to understand can participate, and their needs can be met.

Richard Baxter was a great man of God who took a very wealthy and sophisticated parish. For three years he preached with all the passion of his heart without any visible response. Finally, one day, he threw himself across the floor in his study and cried out, "O God, You must do something with these people or I'll die!"

He said, "It was as if God spoke to me audibly, 'Baxter, you are working in the wrong place. You're expecting revival to come through the church. Try the home.' "

Richard Baxter went out and called on home after home.

He spent entire evenings in homes helping parents set up family worship times with their children. He moved from one home to another. Finally, the Spirit of God started to light fires all over until they swept through the congregation and made it the great church that it became—and made Baxter a man of godly distinction.

We hear much about revival today, but it is always in connection with the church. I wonder if perhaps God is saying to us, "You're working in the wrong place." Ask God to bring revival in your home. If He does, I'll guarantee it will infect the church. And I believe it begins when you and I establish a value system—a priority system—to meet the Lord every day with our families. Remember, He's seeking *your* worship.

Recommended Reading for Family Worship

PRESCHOOL CHILDREN

Barrett, Ethel and Blankenbaker, Frances. *Our Family's First Bible Storybook.* Ventura, Calif.: Regal Books.

Henley, Karyn. *The Beginner's Bible.* Phoenix: Questar Publications, Inc., 1989.

Lindvall, Ella K. *The Bible Illustrated for Little Children.* Chicago: Moody Press, 1985.

Sattgast, L.J. *My Very First Bible.* Eugene, Ore.: Harvest House Publishers, 1989.

SCHOOL CHILDREN

Erickson, Mary. *Learning About God from A to Z.* Colorado Springs, Colo.: NavPress, 1989.

Jahsmann, Alan H. and Martin, Simon P. *Little Visits with God.* St. Louis: Concordia Publishing House, 1957.

Lewis, C.S. *The Chronicles of Narnia* (7 vols.). New York: Macmillan, several editions.

Oyer, Sharron; Cannon, Kelly; and Torjussen, Jean. *Seekers in Sneakers.* Eugene, Ore.: Harvest House Publishers, 1989.

Taylor, Kenneth. *Devotions for the Children's Hour.* Chicago: Moody Press, 1954.

ADOLESCENTS

Campbell, Stan. *BibleLog: Thru the Bible Series* (8 vols.). Wheaton, Ill.: Victor Books, 1988-89.

Davis, Ken. *How to Live with Your Parents without Losing Your Mind.* El Cajon, Calif.: Youth Specialties.

Realistic Devotions for Teens (4 vols.). Wheaton, Ill.: Harold Shaw Publishers, 1989.

Ten Boom, Corrie and John Scherrill. *The Hiding Place.* New York: Bantam Books.

MISSIONARY BOOKS

Elliot, Elisabeth. *Through Gates of Splendor.* Wheaton, Ill.: Tyndale House Publishers, 1986.

Johnstone, Patrick J. *Operation World.* Fort Washington, Pa.: WEC International, 1986.

Tucker, Ruth A. *From Jerusalem to Irian Jaya.* Grand Rapids: Acadamie Books (Zondervan Publishing House), 1983.

When People Pray. Robesonia, Pa.: Overseas Missionary Fellowship Books, 1987.

Someone once defined
a Puritan as
"a person who suffers from
an overwhelming dread
that somewhere, sometime, somehow,
someone may be enjoying himself"—
[this is] descriptive of
the muddled mentality
of some believers.

SIX
What to Do When the TV Tube
Burns Out

The soot of everyday living makes the Christian family tend to resemble a cleaning crew. We are forever dusting off our discipline measures, repairing our budgets, checking up on the children's education—spiritual, secular, sexual, and otherwise—retouching our community relations, and polishing our goals.

No question about it, rearing a family properly is a big task; it is physically and emotionally exhausting. So we need times to relax, opportunities to recoup our strength and energy. With perceptive practicality, our Lord said to His tired men, "Come ye yourselves apart . . . and rest a while" (Mark 6:31). Vance Havner said it, "If you don't come apart, you'll come apart."

Ecclesiastes reminds us there is "a time to laugh" (Ecc. 3:4). Listen to this Old Testament editorial: "What does one really get from hard work? I have thought about this in connection with all the various kinds of work God has given to mankind. Everything is appropriate in its own time. But though God has planted eternity in the hearts of men, even so, man cannot see the whole scope of God's work, from beginning to end. So I conclude that, first, there is nothing better for a man than to be happy and to enjoy himself as long as he can; and second, that he should eat and drink and enjoy the fruits of his labors, for these are gifts from God" (Ecc. 3:9-13, TLB).

Family recreation is not a heavy subject, but it *is* quite heavy upon my heart. It may determine the future of your life and family, as well as the quality of both.

Psalm 16:11 says, "Thou wilt make known to me the path of life" (NASB). How unfortunate, then, that Christianity should be caricatured as a way of death! No doubt about it, the enemy has promoted the idea that to be a Christian is frankly a drag. To be spiritual means to be miserable.

Someone once defined a Puritan as "a person who suffers from an overwhelming dread that somewhere, sometime, somehow, someone may be enjoying himself." A rather extreme judgment, but descriptive of the muddled mentality of some believers. Eternal life, the New Testament assures us, is more than a *quantitative* thing, an unending existence. The person in hell will have that! God's life is a *qualitative* thing, a new kind of life. It does not begin at death; it begins at birth—the new birth.

Check it out for yourself. John 17 lists seven characteristics of eternal life, and six of the seven refer to the here and now—present possession. So good-bye to the pie-in-the-sky rhubarb.

This new quality of life begins the moment the Lord invades human experience. Why? Psalm 16:11 gives two reasons: (1) "In Thy presence is fullness of joy." Not just joy, but superabundant supply. (2) "At Thy right hand there are pleasures for evermore." The supply is inexhaustible. These pleasures are as exciting in retrospect as they are in prospect. That is rarely true of experience in the world.

I remember as a wild-living teenager always living for the *next* party. Since giving my life to Christ, my most fantastic experiences have involved fellowship and enrichment with people. And this brings no later regrets. Looking back to what God has done in the past is as exciting as looking forward to what He is going to do in the days ahead. That is the kind of life that God intended.

John Locke, the great humanistic thinker who helped shape eighteenth-century philosophy, offered this idea on recreation: "Recreation belongs not to people who are strangers to business. . . . The skill should be, so to order their time of recreation, that it may *relax* and *refresh* the part that has been exercised and is tired, and yet do something which, besides the present delight and ease, may produce what will *afterwards be profitable.*" (Italics mine.)

It is lamentable that we should allow the enemy to promote this fiction among Christians that if it's enjoyable, it must be sinful. People look at us and say, "If that's what the Christian life involves, there must be a better way! They are dead in the head and everywhere else!"

John 10:10 is an extremely profound verse in a remarkable context. Mark the sharp contrast between the thief and the shepherd. The thief comes but for three things: "to steal and to kill and to destroy." That's wreck-reation! "But"—our Shepherd offers a viable alternative—"I am come that they might have life, and that they might have it more abundantly." On the basis of the Greek text, this can be translated, "life, I mean *really live.*" I believe the only man or woman who has the right to laugh today is the one secure in Jesus Christ. The couple out on the street on the way to a Christless eternity is in no position to laugh. The only person liberated to laugh is the one who has learned true life in Jesus Christ.

We are afflicted with a lethal disease—a spongy view of

the spiritual life. Praying? That's spiritual. Reading the Bible? That's good! Sharing my faith? Better yet! But if I'm playing with my kids on the floor—how unspiritual can you get? The kink in this distorted idea is that it doesn't stack up with what Paul said. He encouraged believers to do all things to the glory of God (see 1 Cor. 10:31; Col. 3:17, 23). The real test of spiritual life is how you relate at the *reality* level. That's life. It's not how many verses of Scripture you can quote or how much truth you can use to club people.

In John Bunyan's ageless allegory, *Pilgrim's Progress*, Mr. Feeble-mind is the counterpart of too many modern Christians. Having been rescued from the giant, Slay-good, he is encouraged to continue his journey with the Pilgrims, but complains, "I am a man of weak and feeble mind. . . . I shall like no laughing, I shall like no gay attire, I shall like no unprofitable questions. I am . . . offended with that which others have a liberty to do. . . . Sometimes if I hear someone rejoicing in the Lord, it troubles me because I cannot do so too."

There are three purposes of recreation you need to weave into the fabric of your family:

1. Recreation Adds Vitality and Zest to Life
Too many people do not enjoy the Christian life; they endure it. It's a grim scene. They really know nothing of the grace of God, that emancipation from the drudgery of living. Whether they are into legalism or license, they are slaves. It is only a grace-pervaded life, produced by the Spirit of God, that's balanced.

The "joy of the Lord" is a biblical principle too little taught and too seldom practiced. Joy is like an untapped vein of rich fuel. The Book of Nehemiah records the remarkable story of the rebuilding of the wall of Jerusalem, and the subsequent revival under the Prophet Ezra. During the dedication ceremonies and celebrations, these leaders read the holy law, and told the people, "Go your way, eat the fat, and drink the sweet. . . . Neither be ye sorry, for *the joy of the Lord is your strength*. . . . And all the people went their way to eat and to drink . . . and to make great mirth, *because they had understood* the words" (Neh. 8:10, 12).

God purposes for His children to have intervals of pleasure and enjoyment. Why do we insist on labeling fun as sin? If I dropped into your house or apartment, the place ought to be resounding with laughter. Often our homes are roaring, but not with laughter.

We have had two graduates at Dallas Seminary from the same home. If I had to pick two men from our alumni who are making an impact for the Saviour, I would choose these products of a humble peach-farm home in California. I stayed in that home some time ago, and came away saying, "O God, reproduce this all over America."

Once I asked one of these boys, "Hey, Ed, what do you remember most about your father?" He pondered my question for a moment.

"Two things—and interestingly enough, they appear to be contradictory. I used to have a paper route, and I had to get up at 4 A.M. I'd go by my father's room and the door would be cracked, and I'd see him on his knees in prayer. That made a profound impression on me. The second thing I remember is my father rolling on the floor with us kids in laughter." What an invincible combination—on his knees in prayer and on the floor with laughter! By the way, what will they remember you for? Your nose in a book? Your face hypnotized by TV? Flying out the door to another meeting? Endless talking?

Think about your life. Many of us are engaged in a program of self-flagellation. We are masochists at heart, beating ourselves to death, not half enjoying life on the basis of our position in Jesus Christ. We are the saddest sort of ads for Christianity.

2. Recreation Relieves the Tension of Life

Are you familiar with the name Robert Hall Glover, the great missionary-statesman of the last generation and author of *The Progress of Worldwide Missions?* He gave an address in New York City entitled, "Things I Would Pack in My Missionary Trunk If I Were Returning to the Field." The first thing he mentioned was a sense of humor.

I almost fell off the pew. "That's not very spiritual," I said to myself.

And then he told the sad story of a steady stream of men and women returning from the field because they had never developed the ability to laugh, particularly at themselves. The paths of Christian experience are strewn with the wreckage of brilliant and gifted people, greatly used of God, but who never were able to laugh.

Recreation means renewal—a process of brightening the often dull routines and burdensome responsibilities inevitable to modern life. We live in a society which is over-stimulated and under-exercised—a bad combination. Pressures build and one must let off some steam. Work does not kill, but unrelieved pressure does.

One of our great tasks in life is learning to manage pressure because we never get out from under it. All work and no play makes Jack not only a dull boy; it may make him a dead one. Robert D. Foster included in his devotional book, *Ecclesiastes*, this poem by an unknown author:

> Slow me down, Lord. Ease the
> pounding of my heart by the
> quieting of my mind.

Steady my unhurried pace with a
vision of the eternal reach
of time.

Give me, amid the confusion of
the day, the calmness of the
everlasting hills.

Break the tensions of my nerves
and muscles with the soothing
music of the singing streams
that live in my memory. Help
me to know the magical,
restoring power of sleep.

Teach me the art of taking minute
vacations—of slowing down to
look at a flower, to chat with
a friend, to pat a dog, to
read a few lines from a good
book.

Slow me down, Lord, and inspire
me to send my roots deep into
the soul of life's enduring
values that I may grow toward
the stars of my greater destiny.

3. Recreation Unites the Family

The early church started in a home. There's no magnet like
a home for purposes of unification. This is the place where
you build relationships. It's very interesting to walk into
the room of a good friend in extreme grief. You've built a
relationship over the years by laughing, playing, praying,

weeping together. Now you don't have to say a word. Your eyes meet, and your presence is enough. Too many young people, when I ask them what they remember about their homes, tell me only negatives; not nearly enough remember happy, enjoyable scenes.

A young adult should be able to say, "Wow! I can still remember when we used to get together and play games. Pop would be lost in it. I used to think, *there's my father, this great big leader, acting silly.* It was wonderful! I knew he was for real." You see, that's what draws a family together. That's the stabilizing influence that keeps a kid from going off the deep end. Don't ever forget it, the fortification of family fellowship.

Every family needs a department of the interior to cultivate "sitting loose." Just as your car needs a periodic "lube job," so the family requires the lubrication of recreation to renew and smooth out its inner workings.

Here are a few basic suggestions. These are working options. They have been used by many, and the results in better family living are guaranteed.

(1) *Take a day off and spend it with the family.* How about family fishing? Izaak Walton, the seventeenth-century fishing enthusiast, wrote, "We may say of angling as Dr. Boteler said of strawberries: 'Doubtless God could have made a better berry, but doubtless God never did.' And so, if I might be the judge, God never did make a more calm, quiet innocent recreation than angling."

(2) *Carve out a daily playtime with small children.* A little means a lot. Study your schedule to determine the best time of the day.

(3) *Designate a family night.* Let the family *decide* and *do* something for fun. We used to have the Hendricks Talent Theater—a homegrown comedy special, always a hit.

(4) *Have a family vacation.* Even a weekend is mean-

ingful when you are saying with your actions, "I choose to spend this time with you." That says worlds about your priorities.

(5) *Try a couple's retreat.* Get away with others, or just the two of you. Evaluate your family away from the scene of action. Set goals. Readjust your priorities.

(6) *Explore interfamily recreation.* Invite another family to your home—just for fun.

Family fun requires a free spirit as well as free time. A free spirit escapes once in a while from the demands of life's regular routine. Jesus Christ warned: "Beware! Don't always be wishing for what you don't have. For real life and real living are not related to how rich you are" (Luke 12:15, TLB). Then He told the story of a prosperous but very foolish farmer. While the point of the parable lies elsewhere, it gives an example of a man who kept running an expansion program until he far outstripped anybody else in the neighborhood. When he decided to take a vacation, it was too late.

At Dallas Theological Seminary we took a survey of some 350 student wives concerning low-cost Christian family recreational activities. Here are some "Ideas to Blow Your Boredom to Bits."

> Attend a hockey game
> Picnic at the lake (watch sailboats, walk along shore, play Frisbee, feed ducks)
> Visit the zoo
> Fly kites
> Go jogging
> Pick wildflowers, leaves, pecans, dried wood, pinecones
> Walk in the country; go for a drive
> Eat in a quaint little restaurant
> Watch TV and eat popcorn

Go biking
Take tours of historical sites
Celebrate husband's birthday with treasure hunt of
    small gifts around the apartment
Canoe down the river
Play table games at home; look at family pictures
Walk in the neighborhood
Visit museums and art galleries
Window-shop
Make tape for family and friends abroad
Play tennis
Walk dog in the park
Make a pie together
Watch planes arrive and leave at the airport
Create table centerpiece together
Go roller-skating
Sing together
Shop and learn about antiques
Make candles
Walk through cemetery and read old markers
Play touch football in the park
Learn archery
Let the children entertain with puppets
Camp out

BONUS IDEAS TO STRETCH YOU

Read aloud
Write "round robin" letter to special friends
Draw or paint
Have family theater with original script and
    costumes
Make a "family tree"
Garden (inside or out)

Learn new crafts (ceramics, woodworking, flower
arranging, rock polishing)
Take a mystery trip
Train a dog
Explore local tours through interesting plants (bak-
ery, bottling company, newspaper, etc.)

Billboards have heralded it: "The family that prays—and
plays—together stays together." That isn't the entire solution to family problems, but prayer and play are worthwhile and indispensable ingredients for the Christian family's unity.

Family recreation can be pulled down off the top shelf of
"things I'd like to do someday" and put in working order
with four simple principles.

Plan it. We don't plan to fail, but we fail to plan.

Vary it. Avoid recreational ruts with all kinds of mental,
physical, social, and cultural outlets.

Provide for it. Budget a little bit of money—a small investment with lifelong dividends.

Think creatively. Put together your own original family
fun-times. Work toward being participants rather than
spectators. Be involved, not just entertained.

Sprinkle some recreational spice into your family's living
patterns. You'll have a whole new ball game!

*Debt can be
a slowly rising tide
that casts an
unsuspecting family adrift
in a treacherous sea.*

SEVEN
Bills, Budgets, and Bank Loans

A financial skeleton lurks in many Christian closets. It appears periodically to haunt and harass the family. Conservatively, it is estimated that 50 percent of the problems of marriage involve finances. Money matters constitute a major cause of divorce in America.

A cartoon pictured a coed chatting with her soon-to-be-wed friend: "I sure hope you have a happy marriage."

"Oh, we won't have any problems," replied the bride-to-be, "as long as we don't mention money!" She was adding to her marriage vows an invisible exception: "till debt do us part." Debt can be a slowly rising tide that casts an unsuspecting family adrift in a treacherous sea.

No home can escape the clutches of coin and currency. Three aspects of family finances are particularly important: (1) biblical truth concerning money, (2) intelligent management of money, and (3) training of children regarding money.

The Bible is full of examples, exhortations, commands, and warnings about money. Greed is everywhere denounced, and generosity is everywhere extolled. Nor does the Bible contain any apology for its financial emphases.

First Corinthians 15 highlights the resurrection theme; then chapter 16 concerns the collection. Discordant? Not really, because it takes resurrection power to get money out of some people! Finances may be the greatest reflection of resurrection reality at work.

The Gospels hook the reader on this subject. Jesus Christ said more about money than about heaven and hell combined. Almost every parable relates to finances.

The warp and woof of biblical revelation concerning money is of four main elements:

1. Christian Stewardship Is Total, Not Partial

Everything you possess is sourced in God. It is not what you do with the 10 or 20 percent you give, but rather what you do with the 80 or 90 percent you retain. Many Christians feel that by giving a small percentage they have obviously bypassed all other responsibilities and can do as they please with the remainder. Nothing is further from Scripture.

I think one of the most devastating errors revolves around much of what is taught under the title of tithing. Tithing is presented frequently as if it were something you do in order to get, rather than something you do because of what you have received.

A testimony from a Christian Businessmen's meeting remains vividly with me: "My business was just about to go under, and I wouldn't have made it. But I decided to tithe. I gave God 10 percent, and from then on my business has been flourishing. Every dollar I give to God, He gives me back two."

That's fantastic! How do you get in on that? I don't know a businessman in America who wouldn't be interested in a deal that guarantees a two dollar return for every dollar invested! That's good human finances, but that's not good biblical teaching. You give to God whether or not you go broke! You know that you never will go broke because you cannot outgive God. James 1:17 declares that every gift originates with God. His major characteristic, James assures us, is His constancy. The only kind of gift He knows how to give is a perfect one.

Paul raises the question in 1 Corinthians 4:7, what do you have that you have not received? Answer: nothing.

Several years ago we lost our dog. That was a great trauma in the life of our family. We raised four kids on this canine, a little dachshund, half a dog high and two dogs long. What we appreciated most about this dog was his response when we brought his plate of food. He would almost leap out of his shiny black fur with excitement. He wagged so much we thought his back end would come off. He sat up so beautifully and "spoke" (politely, of course), and licked our hands—he was smart enough as a dog to know where his gifts came from. That's smarter than many humans.

"Why should I pray? After all, I earned the money with which to buy this food." Really? Where did you get the strength, the ability, the breath you take every minute? It is all sourced in Him, and the grateful one not only recognizes it but gives thanks.

2. Giving Is an Investment in Eternity
In 2 Corinthians 9:6 there is a sowing-reaping analogy. If you sow bountifully, you will reap bountifully. If you sow sparingly, you will reap sparingly. The choice in both cases is yours.

The Scriptures do not teach that money is always and only "filthy lucre." They explain that money is *fellowship* (see Phil. 1:3-5, 4:15; 2 Cor. 8:1-5). It is sharing, communicating, either with a blessing or a curse on its use. I think giving money is one of the most significant expressions of faith, because one must give without the element of sight. Sometimes, to help me see the direct cost to me of my giving, I like to think that every time I give $5 to God, for example, I go without a book or an article of clothing.

Have you ever been caught unprepared in a church or a meeting where they were passing the collection plate? You fumble in your pocket or purse. "My shattered nerves! I'm trapped! Nothing less than a five! What a revolting development!" You take the $5, kiss it good-bye.

May I suggest another alternative? Next time the plate goes by, remember that nothing else you have will endure after a period of time. But through the transmutation of spiritual phenomena, that money given in faith to God is translated into terms of eternal currency. You need to ask, how is your heavenly stock portfolio? How many eternal securities do you own?

3. Regulate Money by New Testament Requisites

A pattern is provided in 1 Corinthians 16:2. Giving is to be *regular:* "Upon the first day of the week." Every time the Lord's Day arrives you have a reminder of your responsibility in giving.

Giving is to be very *personal:* "... let every one of you ..." "... lay by him in store."

Giving is to be *systematic:* It is a picture of a little pile, reserved exclusively for Him. It means that God is at the top of the priority list, whether you ever make the rest of the list or not. Have you learned this yet?

We've all seen Christian people grasping erratically at a means of relaxation in our tense materialistic world. "I gotta do something to relax!" they growl. Recklessly, they invest in an elaborate hobby requiring complicated and costly equipment. A year later they are losing money when no one wants to buy their used diving outfit or their splattered darkroom equipment.

God has a fantastic ability to take our money, when it is gained and used contrary to His patterns, and pour it into a bag of holes. Discovered the leakage yet?

Giving is to be *proportionate:* "... as God has prospered." Every time the Lord's Day rolls around, think of the divine prosperity in your life. That becomes the basis. That would transform our giving beyond recognition.

4. Attitude Is Far More Important than Amount

Mark 12:41 says that "Jesus sat over against the treasury and beheld how the people cast money into the treasury." Why such fascination? Because money cuts deeply into character. It's a spiritual barometer, a far more accurate index of your relationship to Jesus Christ than any other element, including prayer, Bible reading, and witnessing. All of these you can do and be shot through with a self-centered spirit. Not so giving—at least not as described here.

"And many that were rich cast in much, and there came a certain poor widow and she threw in two mites" (Mark 12:41-42). The next time I hear about "the widow's mite," I'm going to scream! Bless her heart, she didn't give much but credit her for what she gave—*two* mites. They make a farthing, a very small amount.

Jesus called His disciples: "Verily, I say unto you, that this poor widow hath cast *more* in than all they which have cast into the treasury" (v. 43).

It's as if Jesus is saying, "Drink it in! You won't see this very often!"

It's perfectly obvious He was not talking about amount;

we're already told she gave the smallest denomination. He's talking about attitudes. The scribes cast in out of their superfluity, but she cast in all that she had, even all of her living. If anybody had a legitimate reason for keeping something back, this woman did. She gave it all away, and Jesus Christ said, "Gentlemen, that is worth observing."

I can still remember from boyhood that my grandmother, who knew Christ as her Saviour, often repeated a little couplet which sort of dinned its way into my mind:

It's not what you'd do with a million,
If a million were your lot;

It's what you're doing at present
With the dollar and a quarter you've got.

I hear students say, "When I get out of here, I'll give. . . ." That's a cop-out! What are you doing with what you *now* have? God looks on the heart. First Timothy 6:10 says the love of money is the root of all kinds of evil. The snag is not the money but the motive.

Money Management

Like a volatile gas, money must be carefully managed. It must be contained in a leakproof sack and measured out in proper quantities. It must be directed, applied, and accounted for. This is to say, keep records.

Inadequate records are the primary cause of overspending. Nearly everyone agrees that at least a rough budget must be made, but what happens to the "miscellaneous" section? The mad money? Many homes are shattered on the rocks of financial mismanagement. The key to steering through the channel? Agreement. Who should keep the records? Husband? Wife? The question is not so much *who* as *how*. The one best suited, more inclined toward arithmetic and detail work, should assume the task.

The budget should be determined by need, not wants. The black and white, unemotional facts should be laid out: amount of income, places of distribution, the agreed-upon value system. In our family, for example, we have always leaned toward education in our priorities. We will go without something else in order to buy significant reading material or pay school tuition. My wife finished her college degree after we had four children. The only way we could work it out was through her attendance at a private university with a substantial tuition rate. We budgeted that tuition because we agreed that her degree was more important at that particular time than a new car, or a bigger house, or nicer, latest-style clothes.

Budgets should flow from family prayer, family planning, and periodic evaluation. Christ said, "Where your treasure is, there will your heart be" (Luke 12:34). We likely would have written it in the reverse: "It's just common sense—where your affections reside, your money will be pressing in close behind." The young lover buys his girlfriend flowers or jewelry. The sportsman mortgages his income for several years for an imposing boat. But Christ knows the human heart. He asks for an act of the will *first.*

Does it sometimes bother you when you are praying that many Christian enterprises around the world languish while Christians live in luxury? It is not our place to judge our brother who may have a higher standard of living than our own. But it is appropriate to ask, what are we ourselves doing without, so that the Gospel might be spread and believers strengthened?

Of one thing Christians can be sure. God has promised to supply *all* our needs. He who fed 5,000 and turned water into wine for the thirsty wedding guests will provide for us.

Sometimes, however, He may also let us suffer lack of resources because of our failure to obey His command: "Give ye them to eat."

Giving develops the giver. That is one reason God ordained that His work be financed by the gifts of His people. Our Lord is not only our Supplier; He is also our Investment Counselor with infallible financial advice. Following Him won't guarantee a healthy dollar profit, but it will guarantee healthy spiritual dividends.

Agree to keep a light hold on money. Fence it in its place. Keep short accounts and assign proper priorities.

Don't believe all the ads. Professional home economists report that the most thorny matters relating to money for young people are rooted in advertising. That is a good word of warning. Stick with your decision once you've made it. Avoid comparing and coveting. Don't feel sorry for yourself. Face up to the limits of your resources, your anticipated income, and then decide what you can do without. Flee unnecessary luxuries. A money management expert once advised, "Don't try to climb the Himalayas when your income is better suited to the Adirondacks."

List your needs, survey your situation, and draw up a rough budget. Set your major goals by mutual consent. Credit policies? Decide with mutual understanding.

Do a periodic review. When all is said and done, expect the miraculous from God—not from yourself. Be ready to give an account of your financial state. Give generously to those in need, with a willing and a trusting spirit, if God asks you to do it. You cannot force God's provision. Allow Him to teach you the lessons He has for you.

Evangelist Luis Palau tells how he was particularly moved by a crucial need he learned about while traveling. He went home and told his wife that he had pledged $1,000 during the next year for this need. From a missionary's personal budget this was a staggering sum! Together the Palaus prayed and agreed to trust the Lord for the amount. During the year in a most unexpected way, they received a legacy from a family member in that very amount—completely unforeseen! God always honors the faith of the one who steps out in His will.

Training Children to Handle Money

Children soak up parental attitudes toward money like a blotter. You begin very early as a parent to model what they will be doing years later. I remember my father used to ask: "Do you think money grows on trees?" Most children think it grows on Dad!

The first few nickels and dimes make lasting impressions. Children should have allowances for which they are accountable. There will be casualties.

I remember our daughter Barb desperately wanted to buy cheap, variety store pearls—mostly because the girl next door had some. Against our advice, she spent her entire resources of 25¢ for the pearls. And the very first day she wore them they broke—all over the back of the station wagon coming home from church. That afternoon she crawled on my lap, lavished me with kisses, and said, "Daddy, I guess I shouldn't have bought the pearls!"

"Really? Why?"

She twisted her face into a disgusted expression. "Cheap!"

That's bargain tuition—25¢ well invested. We see young people dropping out of school. It's not 25¢ any more; it's more like $250. They've never learned how to manage their money.

Don't hesitate to use the law of natural consequences. The child gets his quarter or half dollar, or whatever, and goes right through it the first day. He has to live the rest of the week without all the other stuff he wants—and maybe needs. You're tempted to bail him out. Don't.

Our son Bob had a paper route. He delivered for an entire month, and at the end of the month he ended up $64 in the hole! Can you believe it? I had said repeatedly, as he had ordered his daily draw of papers from the route manager, "Now, Son, you gotta watch that draw!"

He heard me, but he was also careless and probably intimidated by his super-salesman type boss. Did you ever get up at 4 A.M. for 31 days and end up $64 in the red? My son is grown now; and whenever I ask him what he's learned about money, he grins and says, "Watch the draw!" You see, that's a basic principle.

Encourage a child in a program of work and savings. We have never paid a child in our home for doing chores. I never get paid for mowing the lawn and my wife never gets paid for doing the dishes—and neither does any child. But if my car needs washing, I'll pay, because my time is worth more than the money I invest. If my boy comes and says he needs some extra money and wants to wash my car for me, I say, "Absolutely, Buddy." I am very happy to pay him rather than the man down at the car wash.

Encourage your child to get a job—a paper route, baby-sitting, janitorial work, waiting tables. Did you ever wait tables? That's a liberal arts education. (I don't think you ought to have a license to get married until you've waited tables!) What an exciting experience with humanity—especially with the Christians who come and leave a tract with a dime tip! A job gives a child a chance to save. I believe that you ought to teach a child to save systematically. I have discovered that the child who knows how to manage money is also in the process of learning how to manage time, and every other worthwhile item.

A little boy was given two dimes. He was told one was

for the collection plate and the other was for an ice cream cone. He ran down the street and in his enthusiasm he lost a dime down the culvert. Standing there, he looked down and was heard to say, "Well, Lord, there goes Your dime!"

We laugh at that, but that's precisely what many of us are doing—giving God the hot end of the poker. Have you learned what Christ meant when He said, "It is more blessed to give than to receive"?

Parents often conduct
sex education like
preoccupied motorists.
They sail right past the
stop signs and sit like stalled
cars in front of green lights.

EIGHT
Survival Training
for the Sex Jungle

"From copywriters on Madison Avenue to teenagers in the junior high locker room, everybody is talking about sex," Donald Bastian graphically reminds us. "The copywriters sell it big, offering it as a bonus with everything from cigars to mouthwash. The kids play it cool, swapping half-truths with a titter or a smirk. But, truthfully or twistedly, blandly or blatantly, directly or indirectly, everybody is talking about sex" *(Christianity Today)*.

Everybody is except parents, who have the most to say (and give). All too frequently, they are silent in twenty-seven languages.

Moms and dads still stammer, and stir their coffee with a fork when "certain questions" are asked. Otherwise talkative grandparents suddenly have an urge to go call the cat when confronted with the query of how fathers figure into the birth process.

When my wife Jeanne was a very little girl, she was riding beside her dad in the backseat of a car stuffed with relatives. It was a beautiful springtime morning, and they happened to pass a flock of sheep in a meadow. A ram was mounted on the back of a ewe. Jeanne's childish curiosity got the better of her, and she asked, "What are *they doing?*"

She never forgot the response. Not a word was spoken, but Jeanne got a very swift elbow in the ribs. She learned quite a bit. She still wasn't sure exactly what they were doing; but whatever it was, she knew that either they shouldn't have been doing it, or she shouldn't have been asking!

Sexual questions are as normal to children as scientific questions. "Why is there a ring around the moon tonight?" the child wonders aloud. Question-time is teaching time. It is an invitation to step into the child's private thought world—simply, directly, naturally.

Parents often conduct sex education like preoccupied motorists. They sail right past the stop signs and sit like stalled cars in front of green lights.

Why should we be ashamed to discuss what God was not ashamed to create?

Dr. Lester Kirkendall, distinguished former professor of Family Life at Oregon State University, says:

> Most people assume that in the absence of direct instruction no sex education takes place. Actually the parents' reaction to themselves and to each other as sexual beings, their feelings toward the child's exploration of his own body, their attitude toward the establishment of toilet habits, their response to his questions and his attempts to learn about himself and his environment, their ability to give and express their love for each other, and for him, are among the many ways they profoundly influence the child's sexual conditioning. . . . The fact cannot be escaped. Parents cannot choose whether

or not they will give sex education; they can choose only whether they will do something positive or negative about it, whether they will accept or deny their responsibility. *(Learning to Love,* Bird and Reilly, Word Books, Waco, Texas)

We hear a high-pitched voice from the fourth row: "But, Professor, it just isn't done in our family. We don't talk about 'intimate things.' I think it's in poor taste."

Start first not with what you *say,* but with what you *do.* Family structure enhances learning about life.

And you shall teach them diligently to your sons and shall talk of them when you sit in your house and when you walk by the way and when you lie down and when you rise up. . . . When your son asks you in time to come, saying, "What do the testimonies and the statutes and the judgments mean which the Lord commanded you?" Then you shall say to your son, "We were slaves to Pharaoh in Egypt, and the Lord brought us from Egypt with a mighty hand" (Deut. 6:7, 20, 21, NASB).

Just as the commandments of God were (and are) best taught in the home, sex education is primarily and ideally the parent's responsibility and is best communicated in terms of home relationships.

Think of each member of your family as points on the edge of a circle. Draw an imaginary line from each one to every other individual. Each line is a two-way street for learning as the family lives together—learning that forms an attitude toward sex as well as other phases of living. Between parents, between parents and children, and between brothers and sisters, there is important interaction. The family is a built-in automatic teaching device!

Parents provide the model. This is why we say that the best sex education you can ever give your child is to love your child's mother (or father).

What You Need to Know

What do you have to know to get your teaching certificate in sex education?

1. *A child must experience from birth a warm, but not a smothering, affection from both parents.*

Balanced giving and receiving of love is a basic stabilizer of life. Love keeps giving when tired, or busy, or sick, or bored—or what have you. The affection must be spelled out in terms of the child.

As a small child, Jeanne recalls coming home from an all-day picnic, dirty and sunburned. She awakened, very reluctantly, as the car was pulled into the garage. Before her father even unpacked the car, he carried her upstairs and put her in a tub of warm water. He understood that this was no time to play funny bath-time games. In practically no time he had gently patted her dry, smoothed lotion on her sunburn, and tucked her between the sheets. His love and tenderness were emphasized and reinforced with permanent impression. And guess what Jeanne did with her own little tykes after an all-day outing?

Unfortunately, some of the most sincere people can rear the most profound sexual deviates. The homosexual, for example, has been found to have had two prime influences: a domineering, overly possessive and aggressive mother, and/or a detached, hostile, passive father. The combination is lethal. Mark it well—a clear reversal of the biblical roles produces perversion. One study involving 1,800 homosexuals strongly concludes, "A constructive, supportive, warm relation with a father precludes the possibility of a homosexual son." Homosexuals are usually not the product of a strengthening, undergirding home.

2. *Children should be exposed to parents deeply in love with each other and unashamed to demonstrate that love in the presence of their children.*

Love is to be a way of life, woven into the fabric of living—not a glossy finish that cracks when it's bent, but a dyed-in-the-wool hue that pervades the whole home. How do children catch this? Like chicken pox—from exposure.

Jeanne and I were embracing in our living room some years ago when our younger son, Bill, came plowing through the front door with his buddy from down the street.

"Shucks! We'll have to wait a minute," Bill quipped.

"Why?"

"My parents are in there smooching. Aw! This goes on all the time."

"Well, let's go in! Boy, it must be great to have a dad who loves your mom. I don't even know which one my father is—every night we got a different dude in our house."

Caution! Don't evaluate your expressions of love on the basis of your children's reactions—especially if they are teens. "How sickening!" or "Here we go again!" is par for their response, but the impact is on the inside. In counseling, the most tragic words we hear are, "I can never remember once seeing my father embracing my mother." What will you give your child as a heritage?

Young children learn through their ever hungry senses—hearing, seeing, smelling, touching, tasting. Ready-made vehicles for love to use. Mother can hand a cup of coffee to Father with a mute attitude that is frostbitten around the edges. Or, she can say softly, planting a small kiss on his head, "Here, Honey, it's mountain-grown—just right for you." Her actions and her words release an emotional air freshener.

3. *Help each child to identify with his or her own sex while respecting the opposite sex.*

Sex is far more than an act, a process of reproduction, or a biological phenomenon. It involves your total sexuality as a person—what makes a man a man, or a woman a woman. Children pick up attitudes like a vacuum cleaner inhales dirt. For example, the woman who cuts down men in her conversation is revealing more than she cares to admit about her own marriage. Sarcasm has no place in a good marriage. The husband who sneeringly remarks as his wife is looking in the mirror, "That's an exercise in futility!" is pouring sulfuric acid on his marriage.

It is a beautiful and wholesome scene when a woman looks at her little girl and says, "You know, it's great to be a mommy." Teach your children that what they are (male or female) is by the will of God. A feminine or masculine protest will never grow in the sunlight of this positive attitude. Encourage your child to develop an innate pride in his own sex. Magnify your mate before your family. "Man, it's great to have a daddy like ours!" says worlds to a child.

Call It by Its Name
4. *Provide a correct vocabulary; use accurate terminology.*

If you are teaching a little child to make cookies, you do not say, "Now we'll get those thingamajigs out of the drawer to measure the baking powder, and use that whatchamacallit there for flour." You teach correct names because the child needs to learn. With a preschooler, you do not go into the technical jargon about the chemical changes in the baking of the cookie. You proceed on a simple and appropriate level.

So it is with the facts of intimate life. We should name the parts of the body. For example, breast feeding of the infant should be referred to normally and naturally. As the child grows older, he should learn that the newborn actually begins life in a place called the uterus, and when ready, descends headfirst through the vaginal opening. This simple explanation lends confidence to the young child who normally is consumed with curiosity and confused by being told, "You're too young to ask that" and then a few years later, "You're old enough to know better than that."

Bits and pieces of information picked up on the playground can easily be warped and distorted. When a child uses a word or expression that is questionable, a parent should respond in a matter-of-fact manner, "Where did you hear that? Do you know what it means? Let's look it up in the dictionary."

You look it up and for a good reason! Then you can tell it like it is, and make an offer: "Whenever you want to know the straight scoop, come to me; I'll give you the real picture."

Attitude and relationship are far more important than information. The uptight, fear-ridden parent is poorly equipped to help a child. Embarrassment is negative learning. This highly sensitive, personalized subject needs to be verbalized first between the parents themselves. Then discussion with the child is not so uncomfortable. The universal lament of teens is, "We can't talk with our folks."

5. *Furnish sex information as needed with a Christian interpretation.*

All facts are taught in a conceptual context. Throughout the process of sex training, we must be sure to communicate with wonder and mystery. When God made Eve, He put Adam to sleep, and it is still a mystery to all of us how He actually did it. Sexual relationships still remain an enigma, despite the glaring focus of the sexologists' spotlight. Quiet awe with reverence and sensitivity should infiltrate teaching about sex, lest a child develop a coarseness. He may go out using words in the wrong context just to demonstrate that he knows about life. Children need to grasp a holy awe, a deep respect, good taste, and a profound sense of thankfulness to God.

Facts are not enough. Interpretation is mandatory. To provide facts without interpretation enables a person only to sin with more sophistication. Too much of what comes from papers, TV, movies, and newsstands is perverted and distorted. Recently, in a bit of research, my wife and I watched three consecutive hours of TV and counted more than 100 distortions of facts concerning life, love, and family relationships.

Sex involves more than the physiological facts of reproduction, the health concerns of AIDS, and the mechanics of the sex act. It is basically Christian education; that is, what differences does Jesus Christ make in every area of my life, including sex?

Mothers, especially, need to know how to handle questions. A little girl comes running in with "Mommy, where do babies come from?"

The mother's first reaction ought to be one of appreciation. "I'm glad you asked." But if she responds with "Oh, no, not again!" or, "Why do you have to ask that *now?*" a negative concept is born with the answer. After the explanation is given, Mother should check up, "Is that what you wanted to know? Does that help?"

A little boy asked his mother where he came from, and also where she had come from as a baby. His mother gave him a tall tale about a beautiful white-feathered bird. The boy ran into the next room and asked his grandmother the same question, and received a variation on the bird story. He then scampered outside to his playmate with the comment, "You know, there hasn't been a normal birth in our family for three generations!"

Usually the child does not want all of the truth at once. He is not interested in knowing all about reproduction, or the sex act, or lovemaking. He wants only a simple, direct answer, and that is all that should be given. Rule: always tell the truth, but not necessarily all of the truth. Don't tell more than one wants or needs to know.

Avoid shame and guilt. Toilet training can often become a classic case. Little Jimmy, for example, is proud of himself. He runs into the bathroom after dinner to urinate all alone. Forgetting to replace his small trousers, he dashes back to Mommy in front of all the guests, announcing, "I did it—all by myself!" Mother should sweep him up, take him back to the bathroom, and tell him as she replaces his pants, "We always put our clothes on when we come out. I'm very proud of you."

Most every home with boys and girls has an exploratory experience sometime. Little Stevie wanders into the bathroom while his sister is bathing. He bounds out to Mommy with an announcement, "Mommy, she's broken." Suddenly he's learning the difference in the species. That's part of his education; it's perfectly normal.

The needs of the growing child should be anticipated. Young girls should know that "a most wonderful thing is going to happen" as they approach the monthly cycle of a woman's life. The girl will be excited and proud as she shares with her mother the fact that "it finally came." Should problems ever arise, she has a ready-made confidante to help.

A young boy reaching puberty needs an understanding home. Some nights there will be an emission, and he will try to cover it. But his wise mother does not even mention it; she will wash sheets while he's gone, and he will fall asleep that night thinking, "Boy, what a mom! She's a very special kind of a person, sorta in the know."

One lady asked, "What do I do, if I walk in and he's masturbating?" Answer: just close the door. (She should have knocked first, anyway.) At another time, preferably with the husband, sit down and talk with him calmly and meaningfully to explain what is happening in his body, how God is preparing him for something, and he doesn't want to ruin it.

Learning from Life

6. *Correlate knowledge with helpful experience.*

We used to have a honey-colored cocker spaniel who had an affair with one of the young canines of the neighborhood, and she gave birth to her puppies in our backyard. It was an event of first-rate educational value to the children. At first we watched from the family room window; then we moved to a respectful distance out in the yard. Mamma dog tugged at each newborn puppy, licked it from head to toe, and then gave it the final smell-test to validate family odor.

Witnessing all of this was a worship experience for our four-year-old, who looked up at her daddy and all she could say was "Wow!" Capitalize on the many opportunities in nature with the breeding of pets, the arrival of new babies, marriages, and deaths to explain life to children. Visit a health museum. Buy well-illustrated books. See that your children know the score.

7. *Provide instruction and information regarding sexual deviates.*

Children need to learn very early about danger. We do not have to scare them, but to make them aware. They will ask as they see billboards, newspapers, and TV items that provoke their thinking. Willingly discuss drugs, abortion, AIDS, venereal disease, marriage without license, communal living. Inform them that sexual deviates are often predatory, seeking converts. Rides with strangers are a no-no. Mail should be monitored—but not read, only scanned for harmful sources. The law provides means for stopping objectionable literature from being delivered to your home. A normal child, from an accepting and loving home, will have a natural antipathy for deviates.

As a child, Jeanne was walking home from school alone; and as little girls will, she tried to measure her steps with those of a man who was also walking through the park. When they reached a secluded section, he beckoned to her and began to unfasten his trousers and to expose himself. She was not in the *least* interested in what he had to show her. Instead, she instinctively ran for home as fast as she could—a normal reaction for a normal child.

Today merchants of menace are pouring out at an increasing rate lewd material which is incredibly accessible to our children. Did you know that *Playboy* magazine outsells *Time, Newsweek,* and *U.S. News?* It is the top college and high school campus slick. Many Christian families have never found the filter to defend against these noxious fumes that poison teens, especially boys. A lifetime of preparation is the best antidote.

Both parents should be involved in sex education. Don't leave the task to the other partner (usually Mom). Surround your child with good literature, and offer to discuss it. Begin early. Sex education is not a lecture; it is a life. The major problems are starting too late, assuming too much, and providing too little.

We cannot change the fact that the world we live in has diluted and degraded sex and bent it all out of God's intended shape. Therefore, sex education is not an option.

A survey of 1,100 teens sought to determine the one area of contemporary life for which they were least prepared. Their response was that sex was the number one problem!

A teen girl approached me after I had spoken in an evangelical church with this query: "If I use the Pill and don't get pregnant, then what's so wrong about having relations with a boy I love?"

Parents, do we need to know more about sex, or is it a knowledge of love we really lack and need?

The solution to our sex education dilemma is implicit in the Scriptures. The lordship of Christ must reign over the realm of sex as over every other part of life. Paul cautions: "God has bought you with a great price. So use every part of your body to give glory back to God, because He owns it" (1 Cor. 6:20, TLB).

Sex Education Resources

Ketterman, Grace H. *How to Teach Your Child about Sex.* Old Tappan, N.J.: Fleming H. Revell, 1981.

Learning About Sex: A Series for the Christian Family including *How to Talk Confidantly with Your Child About Sex, Why Boys and Girls Are Different* (ages 3-5), *Where Do Babies Come From?* (ages 6-8), *How You Are Changing* (ages 8-11), *Sex and the New You* (ages 11-14), and *Love, Sex, and God* (ages 14+). St. Louis, Mo.: Concordia Publishing House.

McDowell, Josh and Day, Dick. *Why Wait? What You Should Know About the Teen Sexuality Crisis.* San Bernardino, Calif.: Here's Life Publishers, 1987.

Nieder, John. *God, Sex, and Your Child.* Thomas Nelson, Inc., Publishers, 1988.

Short, Ray. *Sex, Dating, and Love.* Minneapolis: Augsburg Publishing House, 1984.

Stafford, Tim. *A Love Story: Questions and Answers on Sex.* Wheaton, Ill.: Tyndale House Publishers, 1986.

Wood, Barry. *Questions Teenagers Ask About Dating and Sex.* Old Tappan. N.J.: Fleming H. Revell, 1981.

God never allows more
than we can handle.

NINE
Parenting without a Partner

Of all the bruises which pain American society, one of the most difficult to care for is the plight of the single parent. *USA Today* (5/31/88) reported that one third of our nation's 2.3 million unmarried couples are raising children. Almost 24 percent of children under 18 live with single parents, as compared with 19.7 percent in 1980. In his 1985 book, *Being a Single Parent,* Andre Bustanoby quoted statistics (*Marriage and Divorce Today,* 8/1/83) projecting that by 1990, 44 percent of all children under 18 will be living with one parent.

For a child who in formative years desperately needs a balanced mother-father home with shared responsibilities, the painful effects of an absent parent will be felt for a lifetime. One father who struggles daily with such frustrations described: "We're torn between our ferocious, protective love for our kids and our desperate, exhausted desire to be free of them for a while. It's a never-ending Catch-22" (David Lambert, *Moody Monthly,* Oct. 1987).

We cannot wish it away; the ugly reality is that homes

without loving parents working together are a major factor of American life. But for the Christian parent there is a provision that fills the critical void in the one-parent home. It is described in this note I received:

I'm a single parent and have been for five years now. When my husband left I couldn't understand why in the world God would allow this to happen. Then one day it hit me! Before, my daughter and I had a father in our house, now we have the Father in our "home." The Lord has given me the best five years of my life— so far! We really are a family now.

How can a lone adult cope with supporting and rearing one or more children and at the same time care for adult needs for fulfillment? I'd like to suggest some chief concerns which must be addressed, and to offer resolutions within a Christian context.

Before one grapples with the needs of children, one *must* settle adult disappointment and defeat. Guilt, grief, and anger must be confronted. The believer has the inestimable privilege of the Holy Spirit dwelling within, God Himself, the Comforter and the Teacher. I think it is absolutely necessary that the parent reserve a few minutes, ideally the first five minutes, or more, on waking every morning to commit the day to Him and to ask for guidance. Take a promise from God's Word and hold it close: "They that wait upon the Lord shall renew their strength; they shall mount up with wings as eagles; they shall run, and not be weary; and they shall walk, and not faint" (Isa. 40:31).

Self-talk has long been touted by mental health professionals as a powerful tool to motivate our actions. If so, a parent's meditation on the words of the Bible can make the difference between winning and losing. To ponder the meaning of such strong words as "Fear thou not; for I am with thee; be not dismayed; for I am thy God: I will strengthen thee; yea, I will help thee; yea, I will uphold thee with the right hand of my righteousness" (Isa. 41:10) is to throw the switch that delivers energy and positive motivation. With His help it is possible to put down self-pity, to deal with negative attitudes from the children, and to face the challenges of a tough workaday world.

Single Parent Issues

Child Care: Every perceptive adult understands that children need capable and loving guardianship daily. Day care is the number one concern for single parents. They cannot be in two places at once, and often cannot afford to pay for the caliber of care they wish for their children. Much depends on the age of the child; much is related to his or her temperament. What may be quite adequate for one will not work at all for another.

Custom-design daily routine. Even tiny tots grasp the concept of being "a helper" when they know what to expect. That "we are a team" is an important idea to teach. Mommy (or Daddy) goes to work; the child goes to school or to so-and-so's house. Be honest and simple in explanations. Try to walk him or her through the routine in advance; talk about standing in line, being responsible for clothing and personal needs, about being quiet during rest time. Above all, try to arrange some little surprise at the end of each day—something to anticipate to make it worth cooperating.

Many parents find a combination of nursery school and home care works best so that there is variety and relief from a sometimes overbearing structure. Opportunities for local churches to exercise creative ministries for young children are limitless, if Christians catch the vision.

It is important to check your safety factor and referrals when purchasing child care. Note teacher-to-child ratios;

familiarize yourself with food services; talk with other parents, and look carefully at costs. Probably the most accurate barometer of effectiveness is the response of the child over a sustained period. Carefully observe what is happening to and for the child. Encourage her to talk and to pray with you about the teacher, the other children, and other details of the day. Lifelong impressions are being formed.

After-school care: So-called "latchkey children" are among our nation's most neglected population. Preteen schoolchildren need constructive supervision. During these years, careful and sympathetic planning prevents much heartache as a son or daughter matures. The key is to develop independence which does not include resentment and spite against the parent. The teamwork concept can be most beneficial if encouragement and lavish appreciation are expressed. Some children are amazingly capable at a young age, but rarely should they be home alone. If it is sometimes necessary, an adult neighbor should be on call to help out in a pinch. Neighborhood YMCAs and other community groups often sponsor after-school activities. The wise parent will check out every possibility.

Depression: When one parent is missing, not only does the remaining one fight a personal monster but the children do battle as well. In single-parent families 30–50 percent of children suffer depression, as compared with only 5–10 percent in two-parent homes (*Single Parent,* Jan.-Feb. '82). Poor school performance, disturbed social adjustment, and eating and sleeping disorders alert the parent that something is wrong. The "sad face" often depicted in deprived cultures is a giveaway. Aggressive behavior and illnesses which are real or imagined seem to multiply. It is all part of a desire to give up, or an inability to handle deepseated anger. Perhaps a nameless dread hangs in the child's mind; most often a lack of self-esteem grows because he is not "making it" in our competitive society.

What can you do? Show sympathy. Even though a parent cannot make it all right, words of love and concern help. It's important to talk about sad feelings, not to make believe they do not exist. Encourage constructive activity. Despondency can be blunted by keeping busy. Never should a child be told "not to feel that way." Rather, the opposite should be offered: "It's OK that you are sad." Then the child should be gently guided into the rudiments of problem-solving. Honesty with one's self and with the situation is the only viable beginning to any solution. The child needs to be shown what he can do, and encouraged to give to God those circumstances that cannot be changed.

Beware not to use too much abstract generalization with children. To "trust God" is a difficult concept for a six-year-old to grasp. The idea that "all things work together for good" is also hard to get a handle on. It is enough to assure the child that God cares and loves and provides. One thing is sure: the child tends to imitate closely the true feelings of the parent.

Sometimes a parent is tempted to explain in detail why a situation is as it is. Especially with divorce, analysis is useless and often only triggers contempt in the young child. It is far better to reinforce acceptance and assurance of love. The important fact is "we have each other."

Absent parent: When children are old enough to remember the parent who is gone, fantasies and intense yearning to reestablish the family unit can sometimes become problematic. Joint custody occasionally works to allow a child to accept his or her situation, but the wise parent will refrain from any derogatory remarks about a divorced spouse. If death has caused the void, it is much easier to explain that God took Mommy or Daddy away. In either case, it takes years for a child to resolve the absence of the parent. He must be assured that it is not his fault.

When parents are divorced, it is extremely important that the one with custody not over-relate and try to make a substitute mate out of the child. Young minds simply cannot bear the emotional overload of a distraught parent who tries to find personal, adult companionship in the young family. Writing in *Parents and Children* (Victor Books 1986), Dr. Grace Ketterman offers three warnings to a single parent:

1. Don't treat the child like a parent. Too much responsibility can hurt the child.

2. Don't use the child as messenger. If the child feels torn between loyalties, he will feel guilty if he does not take sides.

3. Don't let the child manipulate. Both parents need to discipline the child and teach her responsibility.

Suicide: According to the *New York Times* (April 1987), every 1.1 seconds a teenager tries to commit suicide. The writer, James Barron, declared that parents are so absorbed in their own lives and careers that they often provoke feelings of alienation and rejection in their children. When a young person decides that nothing is worth living for, then the possibility of ending life becomes very attractive.

The challenge of building positive expectations is the job of the parent whose child has come to believe life is a drag. Because teen years are a time of developing independence and learning to cope with adult realities, a natural move toward dramatic reactions is seen. Very often having less income than peers at school becomes a dominating issue. The young person cannot adequately equate values and may decide that the best way out of being "poor" is to harm oneself.

Local church involvement is more important to parents during adolescent years than at any other age. For the single parent it is a "must." Attempted suicides are usually a call for help and a competent youth counselor can be the parent's best friend. But long before someone outside the home is needed, the parent should be in touch with the child. Relationships at home are critically important. If a child feels needed and appreciated at home, ideas of wanting out are likely to diminish. Part-time jobs, volunteer work, or any activity which develops responsibility, and thereby a sense of achievement, tend to make a child want to keep going.

School performance and motivation: If a child loses a parent during the period of early adolescence, feelings of security are already jumbled. The "broken home" often reflects itself in lowering school successes. Many studies have shown how the typical effects of this situation—frequent moving and disruption of income—combine to threaten a child's upward educational mobility.

Deal with fear. When worry nags, concentration simply cannot take place. Be factual and honestly assure a child that he is going to make it. When failure occurs, it must be accepted and another try made. Resilience is extremely important in preparing for adulthood.

Hit rebellion at the beginning. Signs of antagonism, which serve only as a mask for anger, must be ventilated. Athletics often serve as a good outlet. Sometimes involvement in music or other school activities can be offered as an incentive to keep a child's mind focused.

Immaturity: A child may occasionally revert to infantile behavior as a way of expressing disapproval over upsetting events at home. The child may go back to infancy, hyperactivity, or extreme apathy in an attempt to reestablish the past. If at these times a parent can "keep cool," the phase will often pass, but it should never be ignored. A steady love and firm hand is required. Sometimes a wise third-party counselor, able to explain Christian principles, is needed.

Prayer: Family worship is the best unifier and ultimate problem-solver for any home. For years I have advocated it, but for the one-parent family this single remedy is possibly the most beneficial. With time usually at a premium, it never seems to be convenient. But even if once a week the parent can gather the family together before the Lord, he or she will have built a solid and enduring base into the home. Children may be uncooperative at times, depending on the mood of the moment. But if they are required to be present without distraction, to hear the parent pray, to listen to God's written Word, and invited to participate with thoughts of their own, nothing else can be so satisfying to the deep desire within them.

One central principle needs to pervade the home where tragedy has struck. First Corinthians 10:13 and Philippians 4:13 teach that God never allows more than we can handle. He promises to strengthen, supply, and see us through. Hurting families should remember that God does not make any mistakes and that He is gracious and loving to those who in humility depend on His provision.

Single parents often feel they are hopping along on one foot. It's hard to stay balanced, easy to become overwhelmed, and perplexing if the possibility of remarriage arises. However, a single parent has a remarkable opportunity to be a hero—an unwilling hero perhaps, but one who can prove that he or she has "the right stuff."

Objectives determine outcomes.
You accomplish that
for which you aim.

TEN
Securing the License
to Practice Family Living

When you first began to turn the pages of this book, you were reminded that the Lord God Himself is the only contractor who knows how to construct a Christian home. "Unless the Lord builds the house, they labor in vain who build it" (Ps. 127:1, NASB).

There are two contributors to the construction job: the Builder (the Lord) and the laborers. Both are important; in fact, both are indispensable. God was the original Architect and Designer of the home and family; He knows the plans. To do the actual fabrication, He uses a select group of workers. The quality of the finished product depends not so much on the *skill* of the laborers (you and me), but upon their *devotion and obedience* to the Master.

It *is* true; you *do* build your home. The foregoing pages have set forth practical, workable directions. But maybe you don't need directions! If you don't know where you are going, *any* road will get you there. Sometimes the reason people feel they are doing well is because they don't know what they are doing!

Know Where You're Going

You walk up to the airlines ticket counter and ask for a ticket.

"Where to?" the agent inquires.

"Oh, anywhere."

That is ludicrous! Yet many of us are guilty of building a marriage and a home without any specific objectives in mind.

Lots of families are like sand dunes–they are formed by influences, not purposes. Paul writes, "Let every man take heed *how* he buildeth" (1 Cor. 3:10). But men continue to build their sand castles only to find them inundated by the incoming tide of societal pressures.

It's not enough just being a parent and having children. God has a plan and a purpose for us to fulfill. I was preaching in a church one time when I noticed a little sign on the pulpit facing me: "What in the world are you trying to do to these people?"

I was a bit jolted, and later I inquired of the pastor. "Well," he said, "I had been preaching here for 17 years when I realized I had no goal, no objectives, in my preaching. I put up that sign to remind myself to have aims and to stick to them."

When we lose sight of our goals, we concentrate on our motions. Like the pilot who announced to his passengers, "I'm afraid we are lost, but cheer up; we are making good time."

We cannot solve our problems unless we can see them. Proverbs 27:23 (NASB) encourages vigilance: "Know well the condition of your flocks." And the New Testament frequently reminds us to know what's going on. "Let each one examine his own work" (Gal. 6:4, NASB). "Examine yourselves" (2 Cor. 13:5). The Bible teaches a spiritual quality control for the purpose of producing a superior product.

I visited an office one time where there was a sign: "In ten years what will you wish you had done today? DO IT NOW!" That's good advice for the Christian home builder. We need to form a mental image *now* of what we want for our home and children ten years from now.

Objectives determine outcomes. You accomplish that for which you aim. Aristotle said: "Like archers, we shall stand a far greater chance of hitting the target, if we can see it."

I have never met a couple who *planned* a mediocre marriage and family. Just keep drifting, however, and you may have the dubious distinction of producing one. A mediocre marriage is the result of good intentions but poor implementation.

A businessman told me his company was spending thousands of dollars in planning for the direction of the firm until the year 2000. The same man had failed to spend one hour thinking about the focus of his family's future. Realizing this omission, he took his wife to a Holiday Inn for a weekend, and there they prayed about, discussed, and planned what they were aiming for in their family.

What *do we want?* Do we really want it enough to pay the price? Without goals we do not grow—we grope. "A goal is more than a dream; it is a dream being acted upon. It is more than a hazy, 'Oh, I wish I could. . . .' A goal is a clear 'This is what I'm working toward,'" wrote David J. Schwartz (*The Magic of Thinking Big*).

Richard Bach's best-selling fiction portrays his hero, Jonathan Livingston Seagull, in the opening paragraphs as a loner, developing absurd flying skills. "Why, Jon, *why?*" his mother asked. "Why is it so hard to be like the rest of the flock? Why don't you eat? Son, you're bone and feathers!"

"I don't mind being bone and feathers, Mom. I just want to know what I can do in the air and what I can't, that's all. I just want to know."

This exchange captures the spirit of youth, and the spirit of the family that is reaching out toward the future. "The important thing," said Dave Mahoney, "is not where you were or where you are, but where you want to get." No one accomplishes more than he sets out to attempt.

Niagara Falls is simply a phenomenon of nature—tons of water pouring over a dramatic drop in the earth's surface—*unless* that energy is harnessed, unless a hydroelectric plant seizes upon the power and puts it to work. The family generates limitless resources which may go unused and unchanneled unless parents skillfully enlist them for definite purposes. As believers in Jesus Christ, make your attitudes your allies.

It is altogether possible that some who have been reading these pages are completely disheartened. Never before have you known that God made such provision for parents. Never before have you heard answers to the questions you've had about your home. Your children may have grown up far from your hopes and dreams for them. You may go away from reading this book, saying, "Sorry, it's too late for me." Are you frustrated? Are you running scared? As a parent, are you paralyzed with fear? If so, you can be certain of one thing—you never got that from God. He's not in the business of dispensing doubt and dismay.

I have a comforting capsule of Scripture, a parental pillow—2 Timothy 1:7: "For God has not given us the spirit of fear, but of power, and of love, and of a sound mind."

God denies that He is ever the source of terror, which produces cowardice. God gives three things without which we will never pull off our parental roles:

1. Competence
Power, ability, enablement—that which you don't have, but desperately need can come from God. I find that a parent's

competence is in direct proportion to the age of his children. For twelve years you can do nothing wrong. Suddenly, you can do nothing right. Frantically you cry, "What happened?" When your child becomes an adolescent you either develop a sense of dependence—and humor—or you go neurotic! The problem with being a parent is that when you finally feel competent, you're out of a job!

No one is competent, except Christ. The sooner you come to grips with the reality that your need is not partial, but total, the sooner you begin to enjoy and enhance your parental role.

People often exclaim in my office, "I'm not competent to be a parent!"

Frequently, I jar them by replying, "You're not supposed to be. If Christ isn't sufficient for your need, I've got news for you—you've had it!"

"This priceless treasure we hold, so to speak, in a common earthenware jar—to show that the splendid power of it belongs to God and not to us. We are handicapped on all sides, but we are never frustrated; we are puzzled, but never in despair. We are persecuted, but we never have to stand it alone: we may be knocked down but we are never knocked out! Every day we experience something of the death of the Lord Jesus, so that we may also know the power of the life of Jesus in these bodies of ours" (2 Cor. 4:7-10, PH).

Notice that it is "a common earthenware jar"—just a peanut butter jar to prove to the world that the ability is not ours, but God's.

2. Compassion

God's love is shed abroad in our hearts by the Holy Spirit (see Rom. 5:5). Human love is conditional; divine love is unconditional.

"Stevie, don't do that! Mommy won't love you." You are selling your mother love too cheaply. You always love your child, no matter what he does. You may not like his behavior; but you always love him. "While we were yet sinners, Christ died for us" (Rom. 5:8). God knows us totally, and yet accepts us completely. That's the pattern: His acceptance of you is the model of your acceptance of your child. "We love Him because He first loved us" (1 John 4:19).

3. Control

Self-control is the fruit of the Holy Spirit. The secret of a disciplined child is a controlled parent. Self-control is linked to inner peace—and that is ready for our taking. "Let the peace of God rule in your hearts," wrote Paul (Col. 3:15). The parent who is ruled by God's peace will have little trouble displaying self-control. If Christ is controlling your life, then you are in a position to control the lives of your children.

Competence—compassion—control. These are the gifts God has given. They are also the prerequisites for the kind of parenthood that produces children who are a true reward. Like all His gifts, they are good, and always available because He never changes (James 1:17). We may change. We are up and down, in and out, hot and cold, making it, losing it. God is not mocking us; He is not playing games; He is not laughing, "Ha! Ha! You didn't make it!" Rather, He has lovingly, generously provided all that is required for our needs as parents.

We all desire to send our young men out to slay the giant, as Jesse dispatched David in ancient Israel. This teenaged hero, however, had a lifetime of preparation. Though he was the youngest of eight sons, David knew what it was to assume responsibility. He was out working, in fact, when the big job opportunity came along. Keeping sheep in Palestine in those days was dangerous and often boring. The shepherd had to be resourceful and creative.

David had repeatedly faced and overcome the wild beasts that preyed on his flock. Undoubtedly he had known fear and uncertainty. But alone he had resisted, withstood, and killed with his bare hands the mountain animals. He had become physically strong and adept. In the long hours, he had practiced his musical skills to a point of competence. Most important, he had internalized the teaching of his father about the might and majesty of Jehovah. There was no ambivalence on David's part when he volunteered for the showdown with Goliath. He knew *what* he believed and *why* he believed it.

To help you conduct your own personal self-examination of your performance as parents and homemakers, the following rate sheets are included. They can help you to apply this book's principles for building a harmonious Christian home.

Worksheet for Mothers
1. Are you nice to come home to? When you are away, does the family look forward to your return with anticipation? Think of three reasons why they do—or should.
2. You must keep up-to-date on the current worries and joys of each family member. How can you do this naturally without "prying"?
3. How can you analyze the emotional needs of each family member?
4. Though the father is the spiritual head of the home, what contributions can you make to the spiritual health of your home?
5. What do you do specifically to keep yourself in good health?

6. What personal interests outside the home and family have you cultivated?
7. What steps do you take to keep communication open between yourself and your husband?
8. How do you handle discipline problems when your husband is away?
9. The Bible makes reference to "kindness" and a "meek and quiet spirit" as desirable attributes of a mother and wife. How do you foster this atmosphere in your home?
10. What are you doing to prepare your children and yourself for future problems of separation and realities of young adult life?

Worksheet for Fathers

1. Are you more positive or negative? Do your children think of you as a "don't do that" person or a "let's do this" person?
2. In what way(s) do you actively teach your children scriptural principles of living (e.g., the fruit of the Spirit: love, joy, peace, longsuffering)?
3. Are your children proud of you? Cite a recent example of when they lost some respect for you, and how you did or can correct it.
4. In what ways do you respect the individual rights of each member of your family?
5. When you correct a child for wrongdoing, do you really try to understand *why* he did *what* he did?
6. You are, no doubt, keenly aware that you are responsible to God for the behavior of your children. What are you doing to make them aware of this fact?
7. What action do you take to show your children the same love and forgiveness that God shows you?
8. List five ways in which you could or do assert leadership in your home.

9. What practical means do you use to communicate love to your children?
10. Review in your mind the evidences of change in your life which the Holy Spirit has brought about. Now name two more areas where you want Him to work beginning *now*.

Family Goals

1. What areas of our home life need the most improvement?
2. What specific accomplishments do we want to make individually? (Each family member makes own list; e.g., changes in attitude, decisions to be made, specific projects, etc.)
3. What *family* goals shall we set? (e.g., use of time, socially, spiritually, etc.)
4. What changes will have to be made to accomplish these goals?
5. What are the problems or hindrances in attaining these goals?
6. What is the divine promise in Philippians 4:19? How does this promise relate to our plans?

Suggestions for Remodeling Your House into a Home

Review the status of each member of the household to see that everyone feels he is a VIP in the family. He can believe in himself because this "in" group where he lives likes him, accepts him, and trusts him for himself.

Check the basic structure. Dad is to be the head, Mother transparently supporting him, and the children all sharing responsibilities.

Scrutinize family values. A dominant, unifying focal theme is needed. Anything other than Jesus Christ is too weak for permanent cohesion. A personal commitment to

Christ, backed up with positive reasons, should be the parental example. At some point, every member should be privately confronted with the claims of Christ on his or her life.

Develop family pride through accomplishment with skill and talent. Plant the seeds with music lessons, hobbies, good books. Use every ability God gave you.

Build up the fun side of the family with laughter at mistakes and imaginative recreational pastimes. A positive, constructive home is magnetic.

Ease up on forced togetherness. Give each one encouragement to be away sometimes. At home, provide privacy to foster personal relationship with God.

Overhaul the emotional air conditioning system. Avoid charging the atmosphere with tension. Keep the home ventilated with positive comments and relaxed attitudes.

Sweep out old grudges like worthless debris. Forgive and forget the past, "even as Christ has forgiven you."

Renew the outlets, so that the family is wired for positive communication. A free exchange of ideas, without condemnation, is essential. Remember that communication is largely by life, not lecture.

Keep the door open to family friends, allowing the fragrance of a virile Christian home to benefit others.

Expect periodic spills of immaturity and imperfection. Clean them up with firm, calm, reasonable discipline. Plan a "better way" for next time. Let out enough developmental rope to allow each individual not to hang himself but to tie a few of his own knots.

Allow the Holy Spirit to make you authentically like Christ. No artificial front can stand the daily erosion of home life. What you are is far more important than what you say.